DOUG PEACOCK
WAS IT WORTH IT?

A WILDERNESS WARRIOR'S LONG TRAIL HOME

patagonia

WAS IT WORTH IT? A WILDERNESS WARRIOR'S LONG TRAIL HOME

Patagonia publishes a select list of titles on wilderness, wildlife, and outdoor sports that inspire and restore a connection to the natural world.

© 2022 Doug Peacock

Published by Patagonia Works

Photograph copyrights held by the photographer as indicated in captions.

"Counting Sheep" appeared in *Adventure at High Risk: Stories from Around the Globe* edited by Cameron and Kerry Burns and printed by Morris Book Publishing/Lyons Press. "Why I Don't Trophy Hunt" appeared online on the *Daily Beast* website.

Hardcover Edition.

Printed in Canada on Rolland Enviro 100 Satin FSC certified 100 percent post-consumer-waste paper.

Editor – John Dutton
Photo Editor – Jane Sievert
Art Director/Designer – Christina Speed
Project Manager – Sonia Moore
Photo Archivist – Taylor Norton
Production – Rafael Dunn and
  Tausha Greenblott
Publisher – Karla Olson

Hardcover ISBN 978-1-952338-04-5
E-Book ISBN 978-1-952338-05-2
Library of Congress Control Number 2021947225

ENVIRONMENTAL BENEFITS STATEMENT

Patagonia Inc saved the following resources by printing the pages of this book on chlorine free paper made with 100% post-consumer waste.

TREES	WATER	ENERGY	SOLID WASTE	GREENHOUSE GASES
167	13,000	70	580	72,800
FULLY GROWN	GALLONS	MILLION BTUs	POUNDS	POUNDS

Environmental impact estimates were made using the Environmental Paper Network Paper Calculator 4.0. For more information visit www.papercalculator.org

1% FOR THE PLANET
MEMBER

FSC
www.fsc.org
MIX
Paper from responsible sources
FSC® C016245

Cover photo: Doug Peacock searching for polar bears in the Canadian High Arctic during the summer of 1991. DOUG TOMPKINS

Front endpaper: The Lower Sonoran Desert near Organ Pipe Cactus National Monument where Doug took many of his long solo walks. Arizona. LARRY GEDDIS

Title page: Desert bighorn sheep in the Cabeza Prieta National Wildlife Refuge. Arizona. US FISH AND WILDLIFE SERVICE

Contents: A grizzly leaves evidence of its passing in a Yellowstone National Park riverbank. Wyoming. THE NATIONAL PARK SERVICE

for
Olivia Peacock Linaweaver

Contents

Previous spread: Wild bison roam the Yellowstone backcountry in 1974. Wyoming. HARLAN KREDIT/ YELLOWSTONE NATIONAL PARK COLLECTION

Above: Where arc the bears? Doug checks a Yellowstone map in the spring of 1978. Wyoming. PEACOCK FAMILY COLLECTION

WINTER COUNT

I log my life by winter counts, in the fashion of the Plains tribes who painted significant events on the inner sides of a bison hide. This might be a battle, a treaty, an encounter with a dangerous creature, finding a spirit animal, or possibly a winter so cold the cottonwood trees split apart. Though the Indigenous peoples tended to mark each year, not every year of my life was worthy of a winter count. Some counts could come bundled in decades with only the rivulets of spring runoff and the emergence of bears to mark the in-between times.

So it was with me. I started a new count in 1968. There was my life before the war that prepared me for a life in the wilderness: a good life full of swamps, rivers, woods, deserts, and mountains. From 1965 to 1968, I worked as a Special Forces medic who attended to too much collateral damage—that cowardly phrase they apply to the pile of small, dismembered bodies after a botched air attack. After March 1968, I applied the anger I had built doing that to the defense of wild things, dimly realizing that the fate of the Earth and her inhabitants depended on uncompromising protection of the wilderness homeland and wild creatures. My war experiences, good and bad, prepared me for the fight; it was a gift. I learned to love grizzly bears.

I also fell in love with the Lower Sonoran Desert, a romance started in the early sixties, but broken by the separation of the war: space and endless, clean vistas unbroken by the forests I so cherished up north. By late 1968, I had two opposing mistresses: grizzly bears in the Northern Rockies and the Desert Southwest. When the bears hibernated, I hightailed it south.

———

It's winter now and I sit in a sun-filled desert wash; a few ground flowers are blooming and the stalks of brittlebush show a rare yellow blossom. I sit several days' walk from where Ed Abbey is buried. This Lower Sonoran Desert country is still considered a wilderness and I miss my buddies with whom I shared many of these adventures: Ed Abbey, Peter Matthiessen, Doug Tompkins, and Jim Harrison. I always dreaded the loss of wild country, so much so that I cared not to live without it. Now another threat, the beast of our time—the warming planet—has edged into the sky and every creature on Earth bigger than a field vole is at risk of decimation or extinction.

And there it is. Back to Abbey's ancient quandary: What to do? Duty, textured in with the joy of living fully and loving the Earth. Except for a pledge to fight to the literal end, I never quite solved this problem. Everyone's mortality is in the lens now and it's not necessarily a telephoto shot.

So, I've spliced together some stories to fill the spaces between the infrequent books I've written. I've omitted extensive writing about the eight epic walks I took in this vast desert wilderness stretching before me. It's the huge roadless country between Ajo and Yuma, Arizona. Or more precisely, between places like Wellton and Quitobaquito Springs in Organ Pipe Cactus National Monument. The core of the area is the Cabeza

Prieta National Wildlife Refuge. I made seven of these walks from end to end and another from the I-8 freeway south to the Mexican border. Each one took ten days and covered around 140 miles, depending on the different routes I chose; I never did the same route twice. I seldom, if ever, saw a human track on any of those walks. All were solo, I carried my own water, and I found more water in the natural tanks every three days or so. You have to know where the water is out there, or you die.

These solitary walks were the greatest currency Ed Abbey and I ever shared. Ed finished one and attempted another even after he had begun to die. So, with three friends, I buried him out there.

Solitude is the deepest well I have encountered in this life, and I found most of it either down here in the desert or up in grizzly country. Introspection arrives easily, blowing off the two-needle pines or on the desert breeze. It's also a human luxury, best indulged in before your children are born. My long west-to-east walks were often taken during the holidays and I had to give them up cold turkey once my kids were old enough to know what Christmas was.

But what trips they were! Looking across a creosote *bajada* toward the nearest water in a distant mountain range forty impossible miles away and then just walking there. Startling bighorn sheep, pronghorn antelope, javelina, and deer, and crossing mountain lion tracks in the uninhabited, seemingly endless expanse of arid terrain. Sitting on a memorial hill fasting and meditating for the entire day. Finding broken pottery ollas of prehistoric Yuma and Pima people.

There are signs of more recent human activity out there, too, most of it graves of the 1849 gold rush hordes and signs of a few miners from the turn of the twentieth century. Of course, since the building of the border wall and the increase in desperate immigrants, many unmarked recent graves have been added.

The one name I have run across out there is "John Moore." I've stumbled across it four times, etched on boulders in some of the most rugged and remote parts of the Cabeza Prieta National Wildlife Refuge: twice in the Cabeza Prieta Mountains, once in the Sierra Pinta, and another rock scratching in the Growler Mountains. I have no idea who John Moore was. The dates range from 1906 to 1912. This is very rough country. Sometimes the water tanks run dry and the summer temperatures soar to near 130 degrees Fahrenheit. Twice, the name John Moore is punctuated by a startling phrase.

The closest water west of where I sit is in the mountains, up seven hundred feet over treacherous scree and ankle-breaking basaltic boulders. Prehistoric people visited this natural tank. A boulder not far from the water is etched with a name and that enigmatic inscription:

"John Moore 1909 Was it worth it?"

A boulder in the Cabeza Prieta
Mountains of Arizona etched by John
Moore. Sometimes his etchings included
the enigmatic phrase, "Was It Worth It?"
DOUG PEACOCK COLLECTION

"YOU CAN'T NEVER GO WRONG CUTTIN' FENCE," REPEATED SMITH, WARMING TO HIS TASK. "ALWAYS CUT FENCE. THAT'S THE LAW WEST OF THE HUNDREDTH MERIDIAN...."

Previous spread: A mother grizzly roams Yellowstone with her new spring cubs. Wyoming. TOM MANGELSEN

Above: George Washington Hayduke and Seldom Seen Smith cut fence in *The Monkey Wrench Gang*. ILLUSTRATION BY R. CRUMB

THE HAYDUKE ANCESTRY

"If wilderness is outlawed, only outlaws can save wilderness."
—Edward Abbey

Even today, the flash of a "Hayduke Lives!" bumper sticker is not an uncommon sight on the byways and in the parking lots of America. For me, this signals a public acknowledgment that the writings and teachings of Ed Abbey still matter. We care about the wild ones and believe that maybe the wilderness is the only thing left worth saving.

How did the fictional character of George Washington Hayduke come into imagining? Only Edward Abbey could know precisely how those particular threads came together, but the part of George that Ed borrowed from the real-life Peacock had distinct origins that were rooted in wilderness and both the trauma and value of recovering from war.

—

The most indispensable wilderness experience in my life arrived quite accidentally in Yellowstone National Park during the decade after I returned from Vietnam. Accidental, because I stumbled into the park's lodgepole pine forest at the peak of a hallucinatory malaria paroxysm (it started in the high eastern Wind River Range, so I knew what was coming) and dreamed of grizzlies that turned out to be real bears. That experience can't be replicated today because of human crowding. It occurred long enough ago that the National Park Service didn't especially think a wacko hiding out in their backcountry was worth looking for. That was the combat vet Edward Abbey met in 1968, and upon whom he later based the fictional character of George Washington Hayduke.

With its wildlife, wilderness, and thermal areas of refuge from deep snows, I considered Yellowstone's backcountry a paradise and wanted to indulge in pockets of it without interference from the outside world. This was still possible in a Yellowstone long before talk of bringing in fast food and the internet to National Park Service campgrounds. It also meant I had to hide out—like an escaped POW might have attempted in Vietnam.

At that time, there was no sane boundary for me between living in the edges of Yellowstone National Park and the fantasy of eluding capture by the Viet Cong hunting for me in the jungles of Vietnam. I had had one close call in Southeast Asia and had yet to shake the nightmare loose. I wanted to chisel the episode out of my life like a malignant lesion. But back then I couldn't. I was terrified of someone finding me camped in the woods of America. I traveled with this irrational fear buried in my backpack while tramping across the meadows and through the lodgepole pine forests. The shrinks would try to provide clunky terminology for this pathology a decade and a half later with the term post-traumatic stress disorder—PTSD and such. In the meantime, I prowled around Yellowstone like a madman,

Doug walks along the Firehole River
in Yellowstone's Midway Geyser Basin
in 1976. Wyoming. DOUG PEACOCK
COLLECTION

leaving no tracks in the rapidly melting snow. I fit the criteria for a half-dozen paranoid categories, all of which I embraced as necessary for life in the wild. It pushed me to the edge.

My contact with park rangers was infrequent and cordial. Sometimes I came out of the woods to fly fish the Firehole River. My favorite bend was the Midway Geyser Basin where hot springs sprang up near the riverbank and younger grizzlies sometimes swam. In October 1968, there were very few park visitors and one ranger used to leave his patrol vehicle on the top of the golden grass-covered bluff and walk down to the river to ask how the trout fishing was. It happened to be great, with big two- to three-pound brown trout rising to small flies. His pleasant small talk constituted my entire social life.

But as soon as I hit the wilderness, I instinctually started sneaking around. I followed deep bison trails cut through the spring-snow cornices in the afternoons, where my tracks would melt away in hours, and saved snowshoe travel for cold mornings over the crusted whiteness. My camps were made deep in the timber, on the snow, or on a small patch of open ground near an isolated tree—places where no one could see them from the ground or air. I seldom kindled a fire, and then only close to thermal activity where the smoke resembled vented steam. My clothing, gear, and tents, most from Army Surplus, were all earth-colored and I carried a white sheet in case a plane spotted me snowshoeing in the middle of a snowy meadow and I had to cover up.

From some boyhood instinct, I considered this invisibility the correct manner in which to engage with the wild. You could conceivably cram a dozen like-minded crazies into a single valley and we'd never know anyone else was around. Treading lightly and silently, we moved slowly so we didn't surprise and run off the wildlife. I paid close attention to all the tracks and watched the slow emergence of seasonal plants.

Early spring was my favorite time because the backcountry was empty of people. Some years, three or four feet of snow lingered under the timber and you needed snowshoes to get around: too early for hiking and too late for skis. By midday, even snowshoes wouldn't keep me on top of the crusted snow and I would wallow forward with a full backpack at the rate of about a hundred feet an hour.

Since I was interested in watching grizzly bears and I couldn't follow them except in early morning across the deeper snows of the meadows, I would often set up on a hilltop near a thermal area. Bears exert only one-fifth of the pressure per square foot with their plantigrade gait as do humans on the snow; while bears walk on top, humans sometimes wallow. During midday, I'd watch bison or explore the small thermal spots for animal tracks and look for hot springs cool enough to soak in. By midafternoon, I'd be glassing the valleys and hills for bears; on warm spring days, grizzlies tended to be crepuscular—active in the cooler hours of dawn and dusk.

Soaking in hot springs or drainages is controversial because such activity in the park is mostly illegal today. But what a luxury those hot pools were in the snowy spring when I'd almost always choose camps in thermal zones with a soakable hot spring nearby. In the evenings, I'd carefully pad over to the thermals, alert to the occasional changing temperatures of fickle springs, and slide in, watching the celestial clock drift in the immaculate skies for twenty minutes or so. Any longer, depending on the water temperature, and you would risk passing out.

Hot springs could save your life in the winter. The closest I came to an emergency was not during winter, but in April when I broke through the ice of a small creek while wearing snowshoes. The toes of the shoes stuck in the mud and my ninety-pound backpack body-slammed me face-first into the frigid water. It took me a quarter of an hour wallowing around in the muddy

Doug pays his respects to a winter-killed
bull bison who died in a Yellowstone
thermal area, 1977. Wyoming.
DOUG PEACOCK COLLECTION

creek to extract myself. By then I was thoroughly cold and shaking. Instead of taking the time to build a fire, I wandered over to a nearby, very hot spring. I knew a corner of this too-hot pool was cool enough not to boil me like a poached trout. I stripped off my wet clothes and slowly slid in. As soon as my circulation returned, I got the hell out, retreated to the timber, and built a fire around which I warmed and dried out my filthy wet gear.

One spring morning, I made my way on snowshoes from Yellowstone Lake north toward Pelican Valley. Tracing well-traveled game trails, I cut through the timber following a series of finger meadows and arrived at Pelican Creek on a gooseneck overlooking the river. Across the creek lay Vermilion Springs, and beyond was a small thermal area where I would look for grizzly tracks.

I crossed the shallow creek and made my way into the open ground. There was the carcass of a yearling bison on the eastern edge. The bears and coyotes (no wolves lived in the park in the seventies) were done scavenging on this one; an older track of a large grizzly lay nearby. I wondered if this was the track of the Astringent Creek grizzly, a large bear that I had spotted years before and that was the greatest Yellowstone predator I knew. This grizzly brought down both yearling moose and smaller bison, ambushing them in the spring on the snow where they floundered; the bear circled on top of the crust and attacked them from the rear, collapsing the ungulates with his great weight, which I guessed to be about six hundred pounds.

Retreating to the timber, I found a snow-free patch big enough to pitch a tent. I lay awake until after dark, listening to the snipe winnowing and later hearing the repeated soft hoots of a great gray owl.

Just before daybreak, the unearthly, tremulous, winnowing sound that snipe make with their outer tail feathers awakened me. I think I will hear this sound on my deathbed—if you didn't know what it was, you might think the meadows were haunted. I got out early and glassed the meadows and hills for bears. Finding none, I packed up my gear and set off on snowshoes to the east, toward Astringent Creek. I trekked at a good pace along the edge of the big valley until midday when the crust on the snow began to soften.

There was open ground near the confluence of Astringent and Pelican Creeks, but I knew it was a rapidly developing thermal spot with swamps, mud pots, and several big hot springs. (The United States Geological Survey would "discover" these hot springs a decade or so later and helicopter in geologists to study them.) I avoided this small area, and turned up into Astringent Creek and got a couple of miles further north before the snow gave out. I dumped off my pack in the timber west of the creek and followed a bison trail as far up as I could easily travel. Almost immediately I crossed grizzly tracks: a mother bear with two yearling cubs, only a day old. In those days, the Astringent Creek drainage was a narrow meadow punctuated with patches of lodgepole pine groves. Subsequently, much of the timber has burned in forest fires.

My problem was that I was on the wrong side of the creek; the westerly breezes would blow my scent out into the meadow where the bears traveled. I didn't want to spook the bears and drive them off. But it was too late in the day to cross the deeper snows of the creek bottom. I set up my tent toward dusk and let the snipe winnow me asleep.

The next morning, I set out early and stashed my pack in the trees east of the creek. I continued on snowshoes carrying my camera gear. I rounded a corner of the creek where hot vents kept the ground free of snow. A brown grizzly of about 325 pounds was digging up small rodents and their wild-onion seed caches. Close by, two yearling cubs watched and occasionally snapped up a fleeing mouse.

The bears were maybe four hundred yards away and I retreated to the timber downwind of the grizzly family. I set up my noisy Bolex 16mm back in the trees with a view of the bears and waited for a gust of wind to cover up the rattle of the old camera. I had taped foam around body of the camera to dampen the sound, but the sucker still scared off wildlife within two hundred yards without the covering of a strong wind or roaring river. It would be years before I got my hands on a modern, quieter movie camera.

I shot a few minutes of film, catching the grizzlies digging along the rodent trenches and gobbling up the fleeing voles or mice, then the bear family moved on up the creek, disappearing around a bump of timber protruding into the meadow. I followed, wading up the shallow creek at a safe distance until the tracks went up a small tributary into the deep snows of the high country. There were a number of big hot pools along this drainage—surprising, because none were marked on my topographic map. I explored for a couple of hours, then stretched out on my pack and fell asleep in the sun.

I woke in midafternoon, shouldered my pack, and started back to my camp. Stepping into the meadow, I immediately spotted the grizzly family back at the same digging site. I didn't want to disturb the feeding bears, so I decided to cut through a line of timber and bypass them. The snow under the pines wasn't deep and the sun had melted out patches of bare ground.

This stand of trees was not much more than a half-hour slog to its southern edge. About halfway through, a stump caught my eye. I looked around and saw ax-hewn stumps and chopped tree trunks all around. There were the remnants of animal-hanging logs. Other evidence lay about: the charcoal of an old firepit, chopped rough logs as benches or chairs, the remains of a lean-to shelter, and broken bottles. I picked up a few of the bottles. They had a rim on the top, a crown top invented in 1892.

Then it dawned on me: I'd almost certainly stumbled across the hidden camp of Yellowstone Park's most famous outlaw. Yellowstone's acting superintendent at the time called his capture "the most important arrest ... ever made in the park."

His name was Edgar Howell and the bust went down like this: In 1893, Yellowstone National Park had only one civilian game warden. Poaching was rampant, especially for the nearly extinct American bison whose numbers in 1902 were down around twenty-three or -four. In the early 1890s, probably only a few hundred remained on Earth, many of them in Yellowstone, near Pelican Valley. The price of a winter bison cape and hide was $300, or about $8,000 today.

Howell operated from Cooke City, near the northeast corner of the park. In March 1894, a Yellowstone scout ran across the track of a toboggan near Soda Butte, east of the Lamar Valley. He and another man followed these tracks on skis through a blizzard south into the head of Astringent Creek. This was a tough trip in winter; I have made the trip twice during the easy summer and even then considered it rigorous.

In Astringent Creek, they came upon six bison hides and heads tied to tree limbs out of the reach of bears and wolves. Then they heard gunfire and saw Howell four hundred yards away out in Pelican Valley. He was skinning a bison; four more carcasses lay nearby. Armed with only a .38 six-shooter, the experienced scout snuck up on Howell, who was absorbed in his skinning job. Even though Howell's shepherd dog was there, the scout, coming from downwind, managed to get between Howell and his rifle and arrested him.

By coincidence, a correspondent from *Forest and Stream* magazine was nearby when Howell was jailed. The magazine's editor was the great visionary conservationist George Bird Grinnell.

Grinnell had roamed the Rocky Mountains for two decades, eventually fighting for the protection of Glacier National Park

Buffalo poacher Edgar Howell, far
right, with his dog and his captors near
Astringent Creek in Pelican Valley, March
1894. Doug located Howell's poaching
camp in 1977. Wyoming. NATIONAL PARK
SERVICE YELLOWSTONE COLLECTION

General George Custer shot this Black
Hills grizzly in 1874. Behind him are (left
to right): Bloody Knife, Private Noonan,
and Colonel Ludlow. South Dakota.
NEW YORK HISTORICAL SOCIETY/
GETTY IMAGES

and the rights of the Native Blackfeet people. In 1874, Grinnell had accompanied George A. Custer and his entourage on a reconnaissance to the Black Hills in the Dakotas. There is a famous 1874 photo of Custer, Grinnell, Bloody Knife (their native guide), and William Ludlow entitled "Our first grizzly." Custer wrote to his wife, Libbie: "I have reached the highest rung on the hunter's ladder of fame." Actually, as reported by my friend and neighbor John Taliaferro in his great biography *Grinnell*, Custer hit the bear in the thigh and another nonlethal spot, and Ludlow and Bloody Knife finished off the grizzly. Grinnell examined the old male grizzly and found many scars from combat with other grizzlies during the mating season. Another friend and neighbor, writer Jim Harrison, based the patriarch of his classic novella *Legends of the Fall* on William Ludlow.

In 1894, the laws governing Yellowstone were lax to absent; all they could do was confiscate the meat and take the criminals to the park's border and release them. Howell slipped out of the slammer at Fort Yellowstone.

Meanwhile, Grinnell editorialized, denouncing the extermination of the greatest herd of animals ever to roam North America and Congress's delinquency to protect the park and its inhabitants. Three days after Grinnell's editorial, Congress passed the Lacey Act of 1894. The law forbade all hunting, killing, wounding, or capturing of any bird or wild animal. Further, it forbade the "injury or spoliation" of all timber, minerals, or natural wonders under federal law. The Lacey Act is still out there today.

———

I need to say something about bison: I consider the bison America's quintessential animal, as important to our hearts and souls as grizzlies or any other creature. My own partisan views are carved from decades of watching bison. All the time I lived in the backcountry of Yellowstone filming grizzly bears, bison were my daily companions. Back in the 1970s, grizzlies were less common; sometimes you didn't see a bear for a week or more. But the bison were there, every day, prancing, rolling, and bellowing—dominating the landscape. Watching them became an ecology of thinking. And these bison were the great-grandchildren—many times great-great-grandchildren—of those of twenty-three wild bison they couldn't catch in Yellowstone's Pelican Valley in 1902. Their kinship gave me immense pleasure. And we almost slaughtered them into extinction right here in Astringent Creek.

These great herds of totemic animals have thundered through human consciousness since the beginning of our kind. Today, I have been fortunate to have witnessed the tip of that ancient iceberg of animal craving when I saw the wildebeests of the Kalahari and the caribou of the Arctic's Porcupine herd. But the most astounding herd to roam the face of the Earth was the American bison of the Great Plains. The numbers we hear stagger the imagination: sixty million bison at the time of Lewis and Clark; a single group of ten million bison taking several days to cross a great river in Iowa.

The given reasons for their demise are the usual ones: Manifest Destiny, European dominion, the need for agricultural lands, or a way to deal with the "final solution to the Indian problem" by eliminating their commissary—the bison.

But there was something different about the way we went after the bison. Unlike wily wolves, fierce grizzlies, or Indigenous people who fought back, the bison just stood there and took it. They were killed for their hides and tongues, for sport, and for the hell of it. The army gave out free ammunition to any dude riding the railroad who could shoot them from the train, leaving millions of bison to die and rot. Bison hunters could shoot a "stand" at great distance, taking their time, killing as many as 120 bison from a herd in forty minutes.

Millions of American bison were
slaughtered for robes, fertilizer, and
sport during the mid-1800s. Michigan.
BURTON HISTORICAL COLLECTION/
DETROIT PUBLIC LIBRARY

None of this adds up to answer the real question: Why did the bison hold a place of such reverence and respect for Native Americans for millennia while European immigrants gleefully annihilated them in half a century? The two cosmologies could not be more divergent. I've never quite been able to wrap my mind around this bedrock contradiction. Our American history books don't discuss this dark quandary that seems to represent the beginning of our Western relationship with the continent's wildlife and the land itself. They are the beasts we never knew.

Sentient bison have a "ceremony of the dead," the same as elephants milling around a fallen brother or sister.

———

I shake off my darkness. The sun is setting and I have to go find my gear and put up the tent before dark. The days are long now. I plow through the timber and find my pack in time to make camp on the downwind side of the creek where I expect the grizzlies to travel. My camp is deep in the woods, but I set my camera on the tripod where I can get a clean shot of the meadow. Snipe, then owls, call me to sleep.

Dawn creeps through the trees, dimly illuminating the timberland. I pull on my pants and boots and creep toward the clearing. I pull the covering off the camera and swing the lens. Twenty minutes later, there is just enough light for filming.

A specter emerges from the north on a route that will pass right in front of me. It is a ghostly gray grizzly, rising out of the mist of the warm creek. I recognize this bear: the Astringent Creek grizzly, the great Yellowstone predator. I've known him for half a decade. He looks old, male, no doubt a survivor of the slaughter of the late 1960s and early 1970s when the park abruptly closed the dumps where the bears had fed for eighty years; grizzlies adjusted by wandering into town sites or campgrounds looking for garbage. Senior biologists estimated that more than

170 grizzlies were killed in a five-year period (1968–1973). The Astringent Creek grizzly made it through those killing years, and perhaps his skill as a predator of yearling bison and moose was related to his survival.

I run the camera, recording maybe ten seconds of film footage. The huge bear pauses just opposite me. He spins on his paws and races back upstream. He heard the camera.

This is the boldest bear on the plateau. Grace has made a visitation.

TREASURE IN THE SIERRA MADRE: 1985

Just south of the colonial town of Casas Grandes, I unscrew the bottle and pass the tequila to the driver of the pickup who already holds a can of Tecate between his knees. He looks like he could use a few drinks. The international border crossing at Agua Prieta resembled a Three Stooges shakedown. The bored border police held us up for two hours until we bribed them with half our pocket cash. Later, at the archaeological ruin at old Casas Grandes, we almost went to jail. Tourists and people like us need to tread carefully in this part of the Northern Mexican frontier.

Previous spread: The Barrancas del Cobre National Park, Sierra Madre, Chihuahua, Mexico. MANFRED GOTTSCHALK/ GETTY IMAGES

The problem was that the driver, call him Scarp, and I told a young man we'd drive him down to Chihuahua City. The kid was a graduate student of a Tucson professor-acquaintance and we didn't see any problem with delivering him to the Autonomous University of Chihuahua.

At the border, the kid stupidly pulled an old Mexican visa out of his wallet. Although a trivial mistake, this act opened the door for the border guards to squeeze us for a few more pesos. This they performed with enthusiasm. It turned out that Scarp wasn't the sole owner of his truck; his ex–old lady owned half and it was technically illegal to bring it into Mexico. We couldn't afford to have the pickup searched: Scarp, after all, was a businessman with a considerable stash of Mexican money duct-taped to the underside of the dashboard and I had a complete set of Mexican topographic maps of the Sierra Madre hidden in the back—maybe legal, but still suspicious.

Before we could get our billfolds out and start peeling off five-dollar bribes, they came out grinning with the maps in their paws: "You are going to work down there," they chuckled with knowing superiority.

They had nailed us. I was down here to document the last grizzlies of Northern Mexico, which would at least annoy the authorities and piss off some ranchers. Scarp was a small-scale smuggler: He planned to hide twenty pounds of good Mexican dope in a spare tire and sneak it back to the States. So we complied with the cackling self-righteous guards and got off with a sixty-dollar bribe, a lot for us at the time.

Next, driving south, we stopped at the archaeological site called Paquimé, an ancient town on the old macaw trading route running up from the Valley of Mexico to here, then five hundred miles north to the Four Corners area in the States where the cliff-dwelling Anasazi had lived a thousand years ago. A small crew of archaeological workers was excavating nearby and

Casas Grandes in the Paquimé
Archaeological Zone, Chihuahua, Mexico.
WOLFGANG KAEHLER/GETTY IMAGES

Perry, the kid, innocently snatched up a fist-sized piece of pre-historic polychrome pottery from the fresh dirt and stuck it in his pocket. This kind of innocuous curiosity can land you in a bad Mexican slammer where you never see the sunlight and the larger inmates might bugger you for two years while you learn Spanish. So, we had another problem with the kid, and we solved it with another infusion of *mordida* for the local police.

Scarp and I held a brief war conference while we counted out our last spare bills. Scarp probably wanted to smack the kid around a bit, but there were too many witnesses. Perry was nothing but trouble, so we left him sitting on the curb near the bus station with his duffle and enough cash to get him to Chihuahua City. Tough love, but we were in a hurry to get on down the road without doing jail time.

———

We leave Casas Grandes behind and head into the heart of rural Chihuahua. We have a map and know the name of the mountain range, but the land here is privately owned, most in huge ranches, and it's hard to get into the heart of the Sierra Madre where we hear the last of the wildlife—the imperial woodpecker, the last Mexican grizzly bear, the jaguar, Gould's wild turkey, and the Mexican gray wolf—may still roam.

Scarp is a big man, over six feet with a boxer's physique—maybe some Russian genes in there. His large, ruddy hands grip the steering wheel with authority as we motor down the narrow highway. Traffic is thin. We watch the yucca-studded landscape pass by. We come over a rise and Scarp stomps on the brakes: "What the fuck," he shouts to the empty desert.

Far ahead, three government pickups block the road. Scarp looks for a place to get off the road or turn around, but the police, or whoever the hell they are, have already spotted us. We have no choice except to talk our way through the roadblock.

I point out to Scarp we don't have firearms or dope aboard, but he isn't listening.

If this sounds paranoid, you don't know Scarp. He is very good in an emergency or a scrape. But he sniffs out trouble behind every bush even when there's not much there. This flavor of hypervigilance maxes out in the face of authority, like at a traffic stop or a border crossing, and brings out the cornered-ferret aspect of Scarp's otherwise charming personality.

We coast downhill toward the roadblock cautiously but not too slowly. You can slice the level of tension inside the cab of the truck with a machete. But at the last moment, Scarp's grip on the steering wheel relaxes and I see him taking deep breaths. He shrugs his shoulders and rolls down the window on the driver's side.

At the roadblock, the soldiers are mostly inspecting northbound vehicles and we are driving south. Scarp is all charm making small talk with the uniforms who finally wave us through.

Scarp's heightened bitterness toward the authorities subsides. We lighten up and pass the tequila bottle again. Down the road, the sun disappears behind the Sierra El Pajarito. It's almost dark when we turn off the paved road over a concrete cattle guard onto a dirt track heading west. We are humbled by the immense darkness, the deep purple of the rugged Sierra Madre, and are aching to climb into her wildness.

In the wake of an assassination of a US federal drug agent down here, rumors of narcotic-related violence run rampant. This is ranch country and some of them have been taken over by bad guys; we don't know which are the dangerous ones. Scarp and I need to cross one of these big ranches to get to the mountain vastness of the Sierra del Nido. It's too risky to drive up to a remote ranch house in the dark, so we retreat, turn south on a dirt track, and camp in a sea of grass.

The next morning, we are driving another dirt track trying to find a way into the mountains when we see dust chasing a white pickup. The truck is heading our way. Steeling for the worst— maybe narco-traffickers or an angry, armed ranch guard—we brace ourselves; we'll have to bluff our way out of it again.

The pickup pulls alongside us and we exchange customary greetings with Ruben Barrio. Ruben is the ranch manager for one of the Leggett brothers who own most of the country we want to explore. And surprisingly, he is a gold mine of information; we think we've struck it rich running into such pleasant frontier hospitality.

Ruben tells us that to get into the wild core of the Sierra del Nido, we must seek permission from Luis Leggett who lives in Chihuahua City. Leggett's father, Ruben says, owned a good chunk of the state of Chihuahua before the 1910 Mexican Revolution took it all away. His land was redistributed and the peasants "ate all his cattle," says Ruben, adding that the Leggetts were still bitter, seventy-five years later, about the cow barbecues. Fortunately, the father had enough money to buy back most of the land including the Sierra del Nido. We will have to go to Chihuahua City to get a letter from Señor Leggett in order to pass through the ranch compound and get into the remote mountains.

We consider this to be a most reasonable number of hoops to jump through to gain access to this untrammeled chunk of habitat in the high country of Northern Mexico. Truly, we have to suppress our almost-childlike eagerness to see this wild country that is reported to harbor the last Mexican grizzly. You would think we were looking for gold.

For the record, Scarp and I have our own personal and semi-professional reasons for wanting to explore the Sierra Madre backcountry. We are both self-appointed endangered-animal advocates: I specialize in grizzlies, Scarp trys to save leatherback sea turtles down off the coast of Michoacán. We write up our travel stories, but that doesn't always pay the rent. Hence, Scarp's smuggling. Like other combat veterans, we don't much care that our battles are unfunded or if the means necessary to wage them aren't especially legal.

———

In Chihuahua City, we call the phone number we have for Luis Leggett, who doesn't answer. We go to his building—the Leggett Building, of course. Scarp chats up the receptionist and is told we can find Señor Leggett at the Hotel San Francisco from nine to twelve in the mornings. In the Hotel San Francisco, we find a spacious hotel suite for $21.

Scarp's Spanish is smooth and nuanced; he knows the rural Mexican dialects, as well as rudimentary Tarahumara and some Yaqui. But he is tired of having to do all the small talk and makes me do the arrangements. In the hotel restaurant, I spit out a few words in marginal Spanish and land us both a thin cut of steak overhanging the edges of our large dinner plates. It's no tenderloin, but rather the kind of tasty, range-fed beef I prefer.

We now kill time before meeting Leggett tomorrow morning. Scarp and I hit the saloon, a large, crowded room with a high colonial ceiling and a huge mahogany bar. We sit back and throw down shots of Herradura tequila. As gringos, we stick out, but not too much.

An older man slides over to us at the bar and asks: "Are we looking for mines?"

"*No minas pero osos,*" I attempt. Scarp winces.

There are a couple of working girls at the bar and Scarp talks up one of them. I could see this coming. Scarp had been living in a Mexican Indian village along the Gulf of California, a relatively chaste community, and was in between girlfriends. The señorita he is talking to is a striking biracial girl, petite but sinewy, and pleasantly shaped. She flashes a crooked smile and whispers into Scarp's ear. In a wink, Scarp grabs her by the wrist and leads her out the door.

The bartender makes a real margarita and I linger for a while, staring at the beautiful wood. I call for the check and retire to the room. A couple of hours later, I am awakened as Scarp pounds at the door. I turn the lock and let him in. His face is flushed and he is drenched in sweat. "I just had to get that out of my system," he says.

In the morning we find Señor Leggett in the breakfast room. He is a gracious gentleman who speaks English for my sake. Scarp shows him a copy of *Reader's Digest*. In it there is a picture of me next to an article about grizzly bears; lacking the proper conventional press and institutional credentials, we want to show this man that we are undertaking a serious expedition. The refined don buys us breakfast.

Señor Leggett pens a short note to the ranch manager and we are on our way. We head back north to La Providencia, where Leggett maintains a family in what was once a grand building to keep out trespassers. "It is now a ruin," Ruben tells us, "though it once had many, many bear rugs." During hunting season, all the gates to the large mountain range are locked. "Only ranchers protect animals here," he says.

We spliced the history of the last Mexican grizzlies together with tidbits of news, old wildlife bulletins, and now rumors we draw out of Ruben and Señor Leggett. Up until 1936, grizzlies watered at La Providencia. Around 1955, a 650-pound grizzly was shot in the Sierra del Nido, says Ruben, "draped over a pickup and driven through the streets of Chihuahua City." Ruben considers this legendary grizzly the last of an era. "They should have never shot that bear," he says. Another grizzly (also called *oso plateado* and *oso grande*) was reportedly shot here in 1966. But most recent grizzly mortality in Northern Mexico has been due

This grizzly was killed in the Sierra del
Nido in 1955, tied to the top of a truck, and
paraded around Chihuahua City, Mexico.
A.S. LEOPOLD

to poison bait set out by ranchers or poachers. Biologists claim grizzly bears were poisoned by the predacide 1080, supplied by our government in the Sierra del Nido during the winters of 1960-61, 1963-64, and 1973-74. We hear this last episode of bear poisoning resulted in six to eight dead grizzlies in the Sierra del Nido. I don't know how much of this is true.

The mountainous terrain here is part of the southern Basin and Range Province. Semi-isolated, north-northwest-trending mountains reach westward into the Sierra Madre Occidental. North and east of the Sierra del Nido lie the Pajaritos and Las Tunas, ranges that provide wildlife connectivity. Ruben says there are wolves in the Pajaritos and Las Tunas, but not bears. He's never heard of any imperial woodpeckers, though he knows what they are. Jaguars are rare, though turkeys are everywhere.

———

We drive west out of La Providencia toward the mouth of Cañon del Nido that dumps out of the mountains into the broad valley. At the ranch headquarters, we prepare to present the letter from Señor Leggett to his foreman. Four cowboys stand around until the boss comes out. *El Jefe* wears a Dr Pepper hat with aviator sunglasses. His manner is stiff and he claims he's never been in the Sierra del Nido and therefore knows nothing about bears or wolves. He waves us gringos through with stony resentment.

We pass through the steel gate. A dirt track leads into Cañon del Nido and disappears. The wind stirs the fresh green leaves on the cottonwoods and the grayer boughs of oaks. The stiffening breeze signals the weather is changing. We look for a place to leave the truck and get out of the wind for the night.

At the mouth of the canyon, we find a sidetrack where we can leave the pickup for a week or so while we explore the Sierra del Nido on foot. It's late afternoon, so we prepare our packs and then set up camp for the night. The open grassy slopes are peppered with oak and mesquite trees. There are scattered red-barked madrone trees. The wind picks up and we build a fire in the lee of the pickup. The snarly spring weather doesn't bother us; we are happy as pigs in shit to have entered the gates of the mountains. We don't expect to see another human until we come back out.

The wind tugs at the fire and sparks scatter in the darkness. A few drops of rain fall as we squat around the fire, passing back and forth a bottle of mescal. We eat beans and tortillas. By the time we think about putting up a shelter against the weather, we are too tired and tipsy to care about the rain, which is turning into stinging sleet. We crawl into our sleeping bags and pull rain gear over our faces.

———

The next morning, we awake to a landscape of melting snow. Our sleeping bags are wet but not soaked. We hadn't expected the snow. But what the hell, it won't last; this is April in Mexico, not Montana. Clumps of wet snow drop out of the trees and drip from the cactus. The green leaves of giant agave plants have triangles of decorative white snow wedged against the stalks. Bright painted redstarts, orange-bottomed bug-eating birds, flit in a nearby yucca, brilliantly contrasted against the green and white: Christmas in the Sierra Madre.

We shoulder our backpacks and start up the gently sloping canyon. A trickle of rising water runs down Arroyo del Nido, fed by the melting snow. We head southwest, into the heart of the mountain range. Tracks of deer, wild turkey, and coyote are registered in the fresh mud. Signs of cattle are present, but the country does not seem overgrazed. Scrub jays scold from the hillside. A few scudding storm clouds linger on the high ridges, but the sun is out, burning them off. The creek bottom is about six thousand feet in elevation here, a vegetative zone where mesquite trees give way to oaks, and higher up the slopes we can see towering pine trees. Mexican juniper and Arizona cypress grow along the creek.

There are some old mine diggings near the mouth of El Nido canyon and I drift over to take a look. I poke around in the tailings. I find signs of mineralization, the green and blue of malachite and azurite, secondary copper carbonates, and some boxwork in greasy quartz. The old geologist in me creeps back; some twenty years ago, I got a degree in geology because I wanted to trout fish and pan for gold in remote mountains, but I subsequently became disillusioned when I found out I'd have to join forces with the gas and oil industry, whose rapaciousness appalled me.

I reshoulder my pack and continue up the arroyo (despite its name, this drainage is a little big for an arroyo). A few miles up the canyon, we spot an old bear scat. We dump our packs under a cottonwood tree and examine the pile of poop. It mostly consists of manzanita berries, probably from last fall. The size of the scat indicates a modest-sized bear, though you can never tell if it's from a big black bear or small grizzly. We find an old track of a good-sized carnivore, maybe a wolf or a mountain lion, but the track is washed out and we can't find the claw marks or tell the toe shape, the distinguishing feature.

Our loads are light from the lack of liquid cargo; we left all the beer and booze in the truck, as we want to be clearheaded and tiptoe into the sierra with a little reverence stashed in our backpacks. After the fleshpots of Chihuahua City, a breath of purification is advised. And in these relatively well-watered mountains, there is no need to lug around heavy canteens.

The canyon is a mosaic of beauty. It's midday and the sun is out. Small patches of snow linger in the shade of oak trees on the north-facing slopes, punctuated by juniper and cypress. We move slowly up El Nido canyon. The topography is subdued, more like a dissected plateau than the deep barrancas of the Tarahumara a hundred miles to the southwest.

We find a side canyon, stash our packs, and scramble up the ridge, leisurely following a game trail up to a stunted summit adorned with cactus and alligator junipers. No hurry, we are here to find sign of wild animals. We look around, charting game trails that disappear over distant southern ridges, looking for wild pockets of habitat away from human-used trails—that's where the rare, man-shy carnivores like wolves, grizzlies, and jaguars might be found.

Our shadows run from us as we drop down the hill with the setting sun on our backs. The country here is mostly open oak-grassland, but groves of three-needle pines are common on the north-facing slopes. Now we hear the distant gobble of a tom turkey somewhere up the canyon. By the time we reach the bottom of the canyon, we hear more turkey calls—yelps, clucks, cackles, and more gobbles.

This is the mating season for the Gould's turkey, one of six subspecies of wild turkey. They used to live in southeastern Arizona where they are now nearly extinct. In the Sierra Madre, however, the Gould's are still locally abundant. In the twelfth century, maybe earlier, the Aztecs took these northern Mexico turkeys down to the Valley of Mexico and kept them in wooden pens. This is the turkey the Spanish transported back to the Old World, domesticated, and bred into the tame, large-breasted birds we eat on holidays. The wild Gould's turkey, in comparison, cooks up tougher but is far more flavorful than the supermarket bird.

We could easily survive out here if we had to, snaring wild turkey for soup and grinding acorns. I roll up this contingency in the back of my outlaw mind while considering the tasteless, dried vegetarian food in our backpacks.

We pick up our packs and find a small flat away from the creek under a large Emory oak tree—a good place to camp. I kindle a fire and heat up a pot of filtered creek water. Dinner is a reconstituted minestrone soup fortified with a couple of handfuls of tsampa. We linger in the firelight, studying our topographical map with flashlights. The stars stare back from beyond the canopy of oak leaves. Tomorrow, we will follow another side canyon south over a gentle nine-thousand-foot-high pass into unknown country that is represented as a large blank spot on our map.

Scarp seems a different species of human in the mountains. The adrenaline-fueled layers of the drug and police world peel off him like the skin of an onion. This backcountry version is quiet, deep, and philosophical. Seeing him now, it is easy to forget that this laid-back bunny-hugger once pummeled into submission the three hundred–pound runner-up heavyweight-boxing champ of the 82nd Airborne Division.

———

In the morning, we head uphill, our packs tugging lightly on our shoulders, following the game trail up toward the pass. The wild turkeys have been vocal since daybreak. During the night, a number of animals passed this way, some leaving their tracks on the moist ground left by the melted snow. I puzzle at a five-toed, inch-and-a-half-wide track with claw marks amid the more familiar prints of deer, coyote, and ringtail cat.

"Coati," says Scarp, again surprising me.

Coatimundis are long-tailed, long-snouted relatives of the raccoon family and are more commonly found in the tropics. But I have seen them climbing oak trees in southeastern Arizona and once, down on the Seri Coast of the northern Gulf of California, I ran into a band of a dozen foraging at low tide.

A couple of miles up the canyon, we find the tracks of other members of the dog and cat families: gray or kit fox, and bobcat or ocelot. You sometimes can't tell one species from the other with a single track. I find a very old horseshoe print.

By midday, we are walking under towering three-needle trees, Apache and Chihuahua pine, interspersed with smaller firs. The needles of the Apache pine are a foot long and packaged in wild bundles—like a Ponderosa pine on acid. We have been following the tracks of a sizable animal. The tracks lead off the pine needles and into the sand by a tiny creek. A large, roundish track is clearly imprinted on the damp soil. I squat to look at it. The track shows four toes but no claw marks. It's a big goddamned cat.

Scarp backs up and looks around. I stand and scent the air; the track is fresh, probably made last night. This paw print is as big as my hand, almost five inches wide. The track is the size that a two hundred–pound mountain lion might make, though I have never crossed paths with a kitty that big in North America. The alarm cry of a shafted flicker comes from somewhere up the canyon.

"What do you think, a big male lion?" asks Scarp.

"Maybe," I say, "but the track's a little weird."

The print does seem a little off: The pad mark is wide and trapezoidal, and the toe marks seem splayed out. Scarp and I are pleased to have a huge predator as company on the mountain, though at the same time, I feel a chill bristle my neck.

"Let's get over that pass before dark," I say to Scarp. With a nod, he picks up his pack and slowly ambles up the game trail. We are now traveling the mountains with a hint of danger in our packs. Our most lethal weapon is my Bowie knife.

The trail climbs steadily upward. We can see the pass through the open forest of pines. It's easy going.

We find a muddy wallow from the melted snow just short of the summit, which we again check for sign: the track of a medium-sized black bear lies next to the very fresh print of the huge

The Sierra Madre of Northern Mexico,
where grizzly bears ranged during the
1970s. At least one last bear survived another decade; Doug found a grizzly spoor
in 1985. DE AGOSTINI/GETTY IMAGES

cat. This time the front track of the feline is a solid five inches with the clawless toe marks far apart. The fresh track carries a strange scent. My confidence ebbs: "What the hell?" I offer.

"It might be a jaguar?" says Scarp. "A Texas hunter brought his dogs down here and took one out a few years back."

I have never seen a jaguar or its tracks, but I know they still prowl the Sierra Madre. Historically, they used to roam as far north as the South Rim of the Grand Canyon and Springer, New Mexico. I don't think they hunt humans, but frankly, I know next to nothing about the largest cat in the New World. Scarp has been around them in Central Mexico but has yet to see the spotted cat in the flesh. Most of what I know of jaguars comes from the movie *The Treasure of the Sierra Madre*, in which *el tigre* threatened to make lunch of Humphrey Bogart.

"Maybe we should find a place to camp off the trail," I say, meaning off these canyon bottoms where the animals travel. They are fairly narrow defiles. In grizzly country, the most important safety decision you make is where you pitch your tent or throw down your sleeping bag. I can't believe that last night I didn't wake up when either the coatimundi or the big cat came through; I sure as hell don't want a jaguar, or whatever it is, walking over my face in the dark.

Although the trail we are following is a game trail, there are a few signs that humans have passed this way: old horseshoe tracks, a blaze on a tree—signs of the occasional miner, logger, hunter, or cowboy. None of these tracks or slashes is fresh. We probably have the mountains to ourselves. At the pass, we veer off the trail and bushwhack east along a ridge decorated with big agaves. The idea is to get away from the jaguar's route a little bit. It will be dry on the crest, but we carry enough water to get us through the night.

As the sun sets, a chill wind blows over the high ridge. We throw our sleeping bags next to a small, red-skinned Texas madrone tree and I light a small fire of oak twigs next to an igneous outcrop. The fire is adequate to heat water for a cup of hot chocolate, but I refrain from building a blaze on the ridge that could be seen from a distance. We now vaguely wish we'd brought along some booze to add to our hot drink.

———

The morning sun catches us early on the bare ridge. Our camp is at about nine thousand feet. There is no breeze. The cries and songs of birds drift up from the canyons below: turkeys, acorn woodpeckers, ravens, black-capped chickadees, and bushtits. A kestrel lands on last year's agave inflorescence.

I take a stroll along the snaking ridgeline, looking for old grizzly bear digs. That's how you tell grizzly sign from that of black bear: Grizzlies dig enormous holes or trenches for roots and rodents; in contrast, black bears might tear up an anthill but otherwise don't dig much. In the absence of a recent bear track, extensive digging would show that the grizzly has been here—and signs of this type last for years.

It's a beautiful day, already in the fifties with clear skies; you can see a hundred miles. The Sierra del Nido is an island mountain range surrounded by high Chihuahuan Desert. Miles out on the valley floor, I can see the green latticework of irrigated farming, probably a Mennonite colony—German-speaking immigrants who settled here in the 1920s. While we were down in Chihuahua City, we'd see pods of tall, blue-eyed, blond men in sombreros hanging out on street corners.

I look out across the line of high ridges and canyons that fade into the haze beyond. A kettle of buzzards soars far below. You can see the tops of distant ridges lined up, separated by drainages, curved like bent bows. I'm imagining a big volcano whose center had collapsed—a caldera. The arcing canyons and arroyos could be fracture rings of the volcanic structure. Much of the Madre is similar, I read, with these collapsed calderas in which precious minerals are sometimes found.

The pass is a low saddle between two higher ridges. You can smell the alligator juniper trees near the top of the pass. We start down the divide to the southern part of the mountains. A pair of mourning doves flushes from the hillside. The ground is drying out and we make good time carrying our light backpacks. The country feels wilder down here, far from any ranch. We find another black bear track. I get out my Navy WWII binoculars and scan the horizon looking for grizzly bear habitat; the thin riparian zone of the valley bottoms and the flat, open tops of ridges look best.

The sun is up. The day will be hot; it's hard to believe it snowed just a few days ago. The trail shows the passage of deer and javelina. There are also cat tracks the size of a bobcat or ocelot. We see no recent sign of humans or their cows. But more importantly, we find no tracks of the huge cat. Our disappointment is assuaged with a large breath of relief. The jays are noisy; a towhee perches in a Texas madrone tree. Turkeys again.

We hit the game trail and descend southward into the wildest pocket of this mountain range. The canyon slopes are studded with wild agaves of several different species, one of which is as broad as a small burro. The pointed leaves of some of these rosettes have begun to narrow at the center, meaning the plant is ready to throw up its big central stalk. That indicates that the agave heart is ripe with nutritious plant energy. If you need a meal, just cut off the sharp leaves with a machete, pry up the heart, and roast it overnight in a pit of hot rocks—make sure you cook it to the soft consistency of a sweet potato. The Apaches, who roamed these mountains as late as the nineteenth century, lived on them; roasted agave hearts constituted over half of their daily diet when they were in season.

Our topographic map shows big drainages trending south-west and southeast before us. Dividing these canyons is a long, mesa-like summit, almost flat on top. It's high country at nine thousand to ninety-five hundred feet in elevation. That's where I want to look for grizzly sign.

In the cool of the afternoon, we hop over a ridge into a bigger canyon, which we follow down to the junction with two more arroyos. In the shade of big live oaks, we find a great place to camp—running water, lots of firewood, and a canopy of towering oak and three-needle pine for shade (and cover from potential snooping aircraft—it's the disease of old jungle soldiers).

The night sky is clear with narrow swaths of the Milky Way floating above the restricted view from the canyons. We treat ourselves to a big oak fire, watching the cast of embers fall off into the coals. Dinner is a reconstituted vegetable soup mixed with dried, cracked grains, and crushed native chiltepins as a fiery garnish. The Gould's turkeys have gone to sleep. We throw our sleeping bags at the edge of the campfire heat and listen to the great horned and other owls sing a night chorus with the poorwills.

I am snug in my sleeping bag, about to fade off, when the nearby yips of coyotes snap me awake. A few minutes later, a deeper, lower howl rumbles through the canyon.

"Did you hear that?" Scarp whispers.

The sierra is silent. Neither of us speaks. After a five-minute pause, we hear an answering howl from the opposite direction.

Wolves! I thought that they would be here.

What riches. We are sharing the mountain range with a jaguar and at least two Mexican wolves. If only a grizzly bear would wander into the fading firelight, we'd have it all: a gold mine of apex predators, all the top carnivores of the Sierra Madre.

In the morning, we brew cowboy coffee over a small fire while we pore over the map and plan our day. We will stash our backpacks in the trees and climb up the steep hillside to the flat, high ridge above. The flat runs east a couple of miles, then swings north and climbs to above ninety-five hundred feet. A stocky Mexican black hawk floats down the canyon. We watch the hawk fade into the morning haze, fill our water bottles, assemble minimum gear, and start climbing.

The ridge lies about seventeen hundred feet higher than the canyon bottom. The side slope is steep and thinly timbered, mostly with oak but also with pine and fir. Underfoot are cholla and prickly pear cactus. We pick a small gulley and begin the ascent, startling a sluggish snake—a red racer, I think. The thin soil is gravelly, and we frequently lose our footing. Reading animal sign is difficult with all the grass and rocks. We pause on a shoulder halfway up the ridge to catch our breath. It's time for a frugal slug from our water canteens.

"Where do you want to look first?" Scarp asks.

"Let's get on that big flat and follow it south," I say. "There's lots of manzanita growing on the broadest part of the ridge and we should find some old berry scats."

I wipe the sweat off my brow as we hump the last five hundred feet up to the ridge, breathing hard near the rim. So far during our trip, we have seen the tracks of four or five different bears; the ones we could identify were all black bears. In addition, we have collected six bear scats (poop). Three of them were grass scats, two of berries, and the other one had some fur in it. But the bottomlands are not the only places grizzlies feed or travel; these high, open ridges offer an extra habitat requirement: security from human beings, which is the most important key to grizzly survival. Nobody comes up here.

Near the top, the country opens up. At least, I tell myself, we don't have to worry about the jaguar up here.

Huge agaves grow close to the nine thousand-foot rim and some of the flora is unfamiliar. My botanical curiosity slumbers, as I am eager to get up on the big flat and look around. We crest the top of the broad ridge and step out on a gentle grassy slope partially covered by low thickets of scrub oak and manzanita. The main spine runs east–west, with long, high ridges falling off to the southwest.

At the summit, we pause and gaze into the immense space, empty of things human. Here is the last great wildlife refuge in Mexico, I think. I glance at Scarp; time to go to work.

Scarp and I begin to systematically traverse the widest section of ridge; the elevation is about ninety-two hundred feet. Some of the flat is open. A thin, patchy soil of moss and cryptogams clings precariously to the open ground. What we are looking for are tracks, scats, or diggings of a grizzly bear. The nearly horizontal part of the ridge is about a hundred yards wide, falling off steeply on either side into the arroyos below.

A gentle wind drifts over the ridge. The cloudless day begins to warm. The eastern sides of the canyons below lie in shadow and I can see a canyon headed out to the southern section of the mountain range. The pebbly ground on top of the ridge makes tracking difficult, though game trails are evident. We find older tracks of large deer and cross fresh sign of wild pigs. No trace of the big cat up here.

"Over here," calls Scarp from down the ridge. In a small clearing, amid a low thicket of scrub oak and manzanita, Scarp has located a pile of bear droppings. I pick the scat apart and identify ants, rootlets, and casts of manzanita berries. It's a big scat, perhaps left by a grizzly.

In front of me is a large hole. It's not fresh; some grass is growing in the bottom. But it could be a grizzly bear dig. A few yards down the ridge, I find more diggings. I wave for Scarp to come over and take a look.

We see different kinds of digs: big holes dug deep enough to bury a case of Tecate, smaller pits peppered into the ridge, and

Doug encountered his first jaguar in the
Sierra del Nido in 1985. NORTHERN
JAGUAR PROJECT

short trenches a foot or three long, perhaps dug for rodents. It's got to be griz—evidence of grizzlies digging for roots, gophers, and something bigger, we guess, to uproot an agave.

My breathing is labored, though not from exertion. This is a huge find. The digs mean grizzlies were on this ridge, deep in the Sierra Madre, last year and the year before. There could be a few left, though probably not enough to make up a surviving population. These are Mexico's last *osos grandes*, and they are going the same route to extinction that grizzlies experienced in California, Arizona, Utah, and New Mexico at the hands of humans in the first half of the twentieth century—killing all bears suspected of conflicts with livestock in a marginal frontier economy where every lost cow was seen as a disaster.

Down the sloping ridge, we find more scat and another cluster of bear digs; we count twenty-nine of them. Rather than guess how these bears might persevere in this land, we bask in our immediate success—the joy of documenting that the last Mexican grizzly survived into the mid-1980s in the sierra of Chihuahua.

By late afternoon, we pack up and head back down to camp, jogging the last mile to outrun dusk. By the time we reach the creek bottom, it's almost dark. I kindle an oak fire and dig into my backpack for the last celebratory food: a tin of jalapeños and a can of black beans.

We lean on our bedrolls by the glowing fire, listening to the night sounds of owls and goatsuckers. A coyote yaps from somewhere down the canyon. Then, a coughing sound, close to camp, breaks the silence. The low vocalization is strange to my ears; it puzzles and alarms us and, for a very real minute, scares the shit out of me. It seems to be coming from a big cat, and that cat is very close.

"Holy shit," murmurs Scarp.

We get up. I throw logs on the fire. The coughing is coming from just beyond the firelight. We are too alarmed and cautious to investigate, so we cling to the blaze. I can hear brush moving. It's the jaguar, for certain.

There is one last cough from the darkness, only a stone's throw from our fire, and then, silence.

Shaken, but also high on this close encounter with the huge predator, we sort out our response. The jaguar is probably just curious, though neither of us is eager to go out and ask the giant cat in the dark what he is thinking. What was this big feline doing checking out our fire? Our camp is certainly in his territory and probably on his preferred patrol route. We wonder what he was hunting; what was he seeking so close to our camp?

Too tired to talk more about this incredible day, we stoke up the fire with oak boughs and lay our sleeping bags very close to the blaze—just in case the jaguar returns for a second look. We take turns throughout the night, getting up and throwing more oak logs on the fire.

———

In the morning, I shake myself loose from a restless night of waking every half hour to listen for the rosette-covered cat. But apparently, he never came back. We step out in the morning shadows to check out the sign. The day is clear and calm.

A hundred feet away, in a dry wash, we find cat tracks—big ones—the same huge carnivore we have been following for three days. I can smell him. Now, the order is reversed, and we are tracking him. Next to a huge live oak, we find scrape marks. The jaguar has sprayed the base of the trunk of the tree, a territorial mark by a male cat.

We pack up our camp and hit the trail. The jaguar leads us down the creek, the cat pads imprinted over our incoming boot marks. We follow the jaguar, and our own backtrack, down the wash to the big junction of three drainages. Every three to four miles, the huge cat leaves scrape marks, and sometimes sprayed scent. At the crossroads, we lose the jaguar's trail, so we trek back north, up toward the summit we crossed three days ago. We are following our route in.

Within a mile, we pick up the jaguar's sign again, leading north. He's walking uphill and we follow his tracks.

By midafternoon, we are near the summit, crossing a small saddle in this rolling high country, still tracking the cat. Beyond the saddle, north of the pass, we lose the jaguar tracks. I backtrack and try to locate where the tracks left the trail, looking for a disturbed pebble or broken blade of grass that marks the spot.

Scarp is weary of my obsession with the jaguar; it's been a long day. We are both out of water.

"I'm going down to the creek junction to make camp." Scarp informs me.

"I'll catch up around dark," I say, "I just wanna see what he's up to. See you in camp."

Scarp disappears down the trail. I find the last seen track of the big cat on the crest of the ridge and follow it west. All fear of the jaguar has ebbed; now I feel like I'm stalking a mythic animal. After less than half a mile, the trail of the cat disappears altogether into a jumble of boulders. The outcrop drops steeply off to the north in a series of gullies. I pull out my binoculars and glass this rugged-looking country. Way down a big gully, I see a dark line, maybe tracing a trickle of water.

What the hell. The jaguar seems to have gone his own way and I need to locate some water.

I decide to bushwhack down the biggest of the three gullies to see if I can find a *tinaja*—a rock pothole drilled into the bedrock by torrential rains—that might hold drinking water. Igneous rock tends to be more massive, homogeneous, and less fractured than other rock types in this range, and tends to hold rainwater longer, sometimes for months.

CHAPTER 2

I step off the ridgetop and drop down into the shadowy ravine. My plan is to find enough water to fill my two canteens,
then bushwhack down the arroyo and back east, picking up
Scarp's trail by dark. A deer trail leads down into the small canyon. I climb down a dry waterfall and see a series of potholes in
the bottom of the gulley.

The first four potholes are dry, but the next has a trickle of
water draining from it. The late-afternoon sun throws shadows
across the arroyo, illuminating the eastern wall of the canyon.
Big granite boulders are streaked and crosscut by white and
brown veins; a few sharp outcrops of red quartzite punctuate
the side of the arroyo. Green agave plants of all sizes decorate
the hillsides—a scene of great beauty. I take a quick break, sit
down on a boulder, and just admire the view.

The afternoon shadows stretch across the wild canyon and
I drop down the steep part of the arroyo. There are potholes
in the bedrock, and in the bigger pockets linger small pools of
rainwater. I climb past a series of step-like *tinajas* until I find a
broad one full of clear water. Digging out a small flashlight, I
grab the canteen cup from the side of my pack, dump the pack
off, and get on my knees.

I've been out of water for the past couple of hours, so I gather a cupful and gulp it down. I savor the clean, cool rainwater,
thinking it is as delicious as a fine wine. Off to the side in the
sand is a very old, large animal print. I can't tell what it is.

But my fantasies run; I feel a racing pulse. It slowly stabilizes,
and then slows as it used to do during ambushes and firefights
in the jungle.

In the moments of fading light, I walk downstream to a series
of bedrock pockets, some with water, some dry—as exquisite as
a Japanese garden. I've got only a short time before darkness
covers my entire route back to camp. A river of cool air pours
down the darkening canyon.

The treasure of beauty and mystery that lingers here belongs to the mountain, along with the last Mexican grizzly. I switch off the tiny flashlight and look up at an emerging planet.

The stars are coming out. I hear a last gobble of a tom turkey safe in his roost. A coyote yaps somewhere in the wilderness. I cinch up the shoulder straps of my backpack and make my way down the canyon in the gathering dark.

Previous spread: The Milky Way illu-
minates the night sky in the Cabeza
Prieta desert, Arizona. JACK DYKINGA/
MINDEN PICTURES

Above: Bighorn rams in the Cabeza
Prieta National Wildlife Refuge, Arizona.
US FISH AND WILDLIFE SERVICE

COUNTING SHEEP

Insomnia has been the central dysfunction of my adult life and I go into the desert to sleep. I figure I have spent almost a year of my postwar life sleeping under the stars among the cactus of the American Southwest or on the desert coast of the Sea of Cortez. My favorite desert for sleeping, however, is the great expanse of country embracing the border of southwestern Arizona and Mexico, the uninhabited desert ranges and valleys of the Cabeza Prieta, one of the best places on Earth to get a good night's sleep.

The Cabeza Prieta is just the name of a block of mountainous hills within an area of the same name now designated as a National Wildlife Refuge. This refuge is surrounded by identical-looking wastelands managed by the National Park Service or the Bureau of Land Management, or used as a bombing range by the military. It's all great country; the only road is Mexico Highway 2 just south of the border. I pay no attention whatsoever to these cultural, governmental, and otherwise artificial boundaries and have democratically thrown down my sleeping bag on about two hundred different nights in washes on all sides of the fences.

The soporific device of counting sheep in order to fall asleep has never worked for me. Instead, I tend to log the constellations with a star chart or read by a tiny ironwood fire until drowsy. Some nights I just watch the celestial clock unfurl or think about a girl I used to know. Sheep never cross my mind until, rarely, just at daybreak when the clatter of real desert bighorn sheep startles me fully awake.

This doesn't happen very often, of course: four times, my notebooks say, four mountain sheep on four waking mornings spread over two decades. Desert bighorn aren't the kind of animal I see very often, although I run across their tracks every time I visit the Cabeza Prieta. The sheep I see, I invariably hear first. One of the best times to do this is in the morning from your sleeping bag, though you can also hear them moving about on the scree and rocks toward evening.

The first desert bighorn I heard then saw from my sleeping bag was north of Buck Tank along a low spine of granitic hill running north into the bajada. I had hiked out there from the freeway. I saw a sign demarcating the bombing range boundary and walked over.

"*AVISO!* WARNING! USAF Gunnery Range. Unlawful to enter without permit of the installation commander. (Sec. 21, Internal Security Act 1950, 50 USC 797.) Equipment, ammunition, scrap and bomb fragments are US Government property. Do not remove. Unauthorized personnel found in this area are subject to arrest and search."

Ignoring the warning, I entered without permit, walked south, and made camp. It was daybreak on Christmas Day in the 1970s, before my children were born. I was still in the bag warming my fingers over the ironwood ashes of the previous night's fire. The sound of rock clattering on the ridge startled me. I reached for my field glasses and scanned the ridge for movement. The slope was bare, with only a few creosote trees dotting the hillsides.

Suddenly I heard more racket and caught movement coming over the saddle. I saw what looked like a gray grizzly coming toward me. The animal's head had a curl of corrugated horn. The bear was a sheep, a ram with a full curl. I dropped the glasses and the bighorn caught the movement; the ram stopped and looked at me from twenty yards away. As sunlight touched the tops of the highest peaks, the bighorn turned and ambled back across the crest of the ridge.

The reason I sleep well in the desert is probably because I walk so much out there. Traveling over the land on foot is absolutely the best way to see the country, scent its fragrance, feel its heat, and get to know its plants and animals; this simple activity is the great instructor of my life. I do my best thinking while walking—saving me thousands of dollars in occupational counseling, legal fees, and behavioral therapy—and the Cabeza Prieta is my favorite place in the world to walk.

I didn't always do so much walking out on the Cabeza Prieta. My first trips out there, beginning in the late sixties, were made in the usual fashion, driving a pickup across the Devil's Highway or easing a jeep up the sandy tracks of the spur roads. Most of these trips and 90 percent of my several dozen non-solo visits to the Cabeza Prieta were taken with two close friends named Ed: Ed Gage and Ed Abbey. Later, when death weighed me down and my domestic life started to unravel, when truck camping seemed tame and I needed a bit of adventure in my life, I decided to walk across the Cabeza Prieta alone. It was a distance of 120 to 165 miles, depending on the route I took. Taking it easy, I usually made the trip in about eleven days—ten nights free from insomnia, ten great nights of untroubled sleep.

In all, I've made seven of these trips, solo backpacking the area from Wellton, Tacna, or the Tinajas Altas Mountains to Ajo, Organ Pipe Cactus National Monument, or Quitobaquito, sometimes vice versa, always by different routes, crossing all the big valleys, which, adding in the early trips by vehicle, means I've spent over a couple hundred nights of my life sleeping out there.

On these desert treks, I average from about twelve to twenty miles per day. The mileage depends on the terrain, if I am fasting or low on food, and if I'm walking during daylight or by moonlight. Anything over twenty miles tends to rub raw spots into my aging body or bruise my feet, especially when I'm carrying my full load of water: three and a half gallons on the longer dry stretches of the journey between the Sierra Pinta and Charlie Bell or Papago Well. My exact daily distance is whatever it takes to ensure the fatigue that banishes insomnia. Night walking is more exhausting because you need to brace yourself against injury; for instance, you have to lock your knee and ankle by tensing your quadriceps whenever you break through the honeycombed earth of rodent colonies.

I keep crude journal notes on all this and tend to record such things as tracks and sightings of bighorn sheep—a big deal to me. I saw few bighorn sheep while actually walking, but as everyone knows, the best way to see them is to sit quietly with your eyeballs at the level of the creosote. I did, however, see a lot of tracks.

What little I know of desert bighorn sheep has mostly been inferred from those tracks, although I've seen a few sheep, too, counting almost three dozen bighorn sheep scattered throughout the desert ranges of the Cabeza Prieta during the past two decades. Ed Gage saw the first one just north of Cabeza Prieta Tanks back in the winter of 1972, on one of our first trips together. He had been sitting on a ridgetop reading Kazantzakis when he heard rock clattering on the slope above him. Gage looked up and saw a magnificent ram with a full curl amble down the ridge away from him, big scrotum swinging from side to side— that's how he knew it was a ram, as he had never seen a sheep

The Cabeza Prieta National Wildlife
Refuge, Arizona. US FISH AND
WILDLIFE SERVICE

before. The bighorn passed down the slope and disappeared below him.

My sheep count of thirty-four desert bighorns also began in 1972 and ended in March 1992. Except for the ones I glimpsed from my sleeping bag, I saw all these sheep in precipitous terrain much like that of Gage's ram. My biggest count was a mixed herd of seven ewes and younger sheep one mile east of Halfway Tank in the Cabeza Prieta Mountains. Once, I saw four rams bedded together and facing out in the four directions on a spur ridge running off the Sierra Pinta into the Tule Desert. I've seen pairs of desert bighorn three times—in the Growlers, the Agua Dulces, and the Cabeza Prieta Mountains. And one time I startled a group of three ewes near an outlier hill south of the Aguila Mountains. The rest of the time my sightings have all been of single animals.

The tracks are a different story. My field notes tell of sheep behavior I have never witnessed firsthand; sheep crossing the big valleys and using the creosote bajadas. I found repeated crossings of the Tule Desert by sheep using the same route during three different years: from the mouth of Smoke Tree Wash east to Isla Pinta. One of these crossings was made by a mixed herd of four or five ewes and two young. Other odd crossings include a ram from just south of Bean Pass trekking nonstop west along the Devil Hills to the north end of the Cabeza Prieta, a single sheep from the Agua Dulces by way of O'Neill Hills into the Pinta Sands, and two sets of tracks starting from an old, human-made pile of rocks on the eastern flank of the Granite Mountains across the Growler Valley and disappearing in the basaltic cobbles of the Growlers just north of Charlie Bell.

You would think bighorn sheep would be nervous out in these flats and open areas where they are vulnerable to predators. I've only seen circumstantial sign of sheep predation twice, and both times it involved mountain lions. Lions are not common in this low desert where deer are not frequently found. The first time I saw lion sign was on a trip with Ed Gage back in 1973 near one of the higher tanks of Tinajas Altas; this consisted only of a recent lion track near a much older, disarticulated skeleton of a bighorn. The other, seen while visiting Ed Abbey's grave in 1990, was a dismembered carcass of a young sheep; there was indirect evidence the bighorn had been cached, and lion scat and scrapings were found nearby.

The only times I've run into desert bighorn—actually I heard them—was at night when the moon was big. Twice I was sitting quietly, and the other time I was backpacking by the light of the nearly full moon. I like to walk at night in the desert. One such night, at the southern tip of the Copper Mountains, I heard the clatter of rolling rocks and the dull clank of hooves coming from high on the slope. This racket had to be sheep moving on the hillside. What else could it be?

Sometimes I wonder how anybody ever manages to study desert sheep; I seem to have enough trouble just seeing them. When I'm up north, in Montana or British Columbia, I see bighorn sheep all the time. I see them in the spring down low in the valleys when snow still clogs the passes and slopes. Later, I watch them feeding and bedding on grassy ridges and avalanche chutes above timberline. Twice, I've found sheep carcasses buried by grizzlies and, though I have never seen a grizzly bear successfully chase and kill a bighorn, I once followed a big male grizzly in Glacier National Park that charged a herd of rams, scattering them up the scree on the cliffs where the bear turned back.

I sometimes linger in grizzly country as late as November and watch the big rams clash, the clank of their hollow horns resounding into the absorbent air of the snow-filled basins and gathering dusk of the Rocky Mountain Front near Many Glacier. I've never seen anything like that in the desert.

One March in the desert, from a great distance, I watched a three-quarter-curl ram browsing south of Growler Peak. I could see he was feeding, but I couldn't be sure on what, possibly lupine. During the spring of 1973, Ed Abbey and I found agave inflorescences in the Agua Dulces chewed off by sheep, and the remains of smashed barrel cactus near Sunday Pass with sheep tracks all around. But what desert bighorn eat from day to day has always been a puzzle to me.

All this sheep lore doesn't add up to much from more than twenty years of observation. To me, the sudden appearance of desert bighorn sheep has always been a mystery, a blessing, sometimes a specter bearing just the edge of fear. Despite my cryptic field notes, my memory of sheep in the past twenty years has shriveled to those who roused me from my sleeping bag or startled me on brilliant nights with a full moon, and those sheep, it seems, I had to earn.

Even sign can be a gift. Twenty years ago, Ed Gage and I found a sheep track outside a mineshaft southeast of Papago Well. Inside the seventy-year-old hole was an old case of dynamite, the nitroglycerin all sweated out and dangerously unstable. Nearby, at Basseric Tank, we found more sheep tracks and the paw print of a lion; suddenly, the entire desert was imbued with unseen power and danger.

During December 1973, Ed Abbey and I drove my pickup into the Cabeza Prieta. Ed and I were unattached and without families at the time. We had spent a sniffling, lonely Christmas Eve at a topless bar in Tucson drinking whiskey. Thinking we could improve on that one, we packed up and drove 150 miles west over Charlie Bell Pass into the Cabeza Prieta. We sipped beer all the way from Three Forks and were a tad plastered by the time we hit Charlie Bell Pass. We got my '66 Ford truck stuck several times creeping down the dark, treacherous road to the well—hanging up the ass end of the truck, jacking it up in the dark, rocking it free—and then dropping down into the Growler Valley. We continued on for one more six-pack around the north end of the Granite Mountains where we got stuck in the sand one last time, and finally crawled into our sleeping bags shortly after midnight.

At six the next morning, a sheriff's search and rescue team roared up looking for some high school kids some criminal son-of-a-bitch had hired to collect 20 and 40mm brass military cartridges. When a helicopter flew over, this bastard had driven off, ditching the teenagers, one of whom, we later learned, died of thirst and exposure. The search and rescue team pulled us out of the sand and went on. Ed and I drove through Montrose Well west into the Mohawk Valley. At the low pass, we found bighorn sheep tracks. Later, on New Year's Eve at Eagle Tank, it sleeted and snowed on us—an unusual occurrence. We stayed three days in the Sierra Pinta, and then dropped south into the Pinacate lava fields, a place of black basalt.

Years later, I followed the tracks of a desert sheep from the bottom of Temporal Pass in the Growler Mountains to the center of the Growler Wash where I lost the trail. I had taken the bus to Ajo after a reluctant Greyhound bus clerk had sold me a one-way ticket.

At Ajo I shouldered my backpack and disappeared over the mine tailings, passing Chico Shunie just before daylight. It was night by the time I reached the bottom of the Growler Valley via Temporal Pass. Even by the low luminosity of the moon I could see big pieces of Hohokam pottery and *Glycymeris* clam shells lying on the desert pavement—the "Lost City" of the Hohokam shell-trekkers. An ancient shell trail ran south to Bahia Adair on the Sea of Cortez and north to the Gila River near Painted Rock where the most common animal-petroglyph motif was that of desert sheep. I lost the trail of the bighorn because of the darkness and because a rattlesnake nailed me in the calf that night.

A bighorn ram negotiates steep and rocky
terrain in the Cabeza Prieta National
Wildlife Refuge, Arizona. US FISH AND
WILDLIFE SERVICE

I had thought myself dead, though by morning it was clear the snakebite was a dry one. The next day, with a story to tell, I walked out twenty-five miles to Papago Well where Ed Abbey and Ed's wife, Clarke, were waiting for me.

Shortly after Gage's death, the man—a mutual friend—who cofounded the Sanctuary Movement asked me to consider "taking over the Southwest Sector." This meant illegally leading small groups of refugees, mostly from El Salvador, from Highway 2 in Mexico north through the Cabeza Prieta up toward Interstate 8, where they could be picked up by a vehicle. Recently, thirteen refugees from El Salvador had died agonizing deaths in Organ Pipe. The work was dangerous, and I agonized long and hard over this decision. I had already begun my work with grizzly bears, and I knew enough about myself from radical politics in the sixties and later in Vietnam to figure out where my talents didn't lie and the exhausting dangers of overcommitting myself. Still, smuggling refugees was something I could do and it needed doing.

The dilemma tore at me and I couldn't sleep. Once again, I went into the Cabeza Prieta to slumber and to track the sign that would show me what to do. The bus dropped me off on the Tacna off-ramp. I shouldered my backpack draped with three one-gallon canteens and staggered into the creosote, headed toward Mexico. I skirted the Copper Mountains, passed Buck Mountain, and at the mouth of the A-1 wash, I found the corrugated remains of a giant set of ram's horns. The next morning, I followed another sheep's tracks south up the wash until I passed over the tiny divide into the inner valley north of the tanks where Gage had seen his ram.

Sooner or later everyone runs into death, and I ran into a lot of it early on. I have used this great desert to bargain with the departed and get a handle on my insomnia. It's true, I invent ceremonies when necessary, especially when my own culture provides none; I erect my own memorials and celebrate my own

Day of the Dead. But mostly, I just shoulder a backpack and walk beyond fatigue across the bajadas, maybe crossing a set of sheep tracks and following them up a wash, and find a perfect campsite. The story of this place is not of loss but of renewal.

The Cabeza Prieta desert is the most important thing Ed Abbey, Ed Gage, and I ever shared, and it is no coincidence that these two desert friends from the past decades are out there. Gage was a tough one because he was a suicide; I maintain a secret, and no doubt illegal, memorial for Gage on a hilltop in one of these desert valleys. Each year for seven years I took a hike to visit this monument and hold a private ceremony.

The last time Ed Abbey smiled was when I told him where he was going to be buried. I smile, too, when I think of this small favor, this last simple task friends can do for one another—the rudimentary shovel work, this sweaty labor consummating trust, finally testing it by lying down in the freshly dug grave to check out the view: bronze patina of boulder behind limb of paloverde and turquoise sky beyond branch of torote. Then receiving a sign: seven buzzards soaring above joined by three others, all ten banking over the volcanic rubble and riding the thermal up the flank of the mountain, then gliding out and over the distant valley. Even years later, I grin as I crest the ridge above his grave, the Earth falls away and mountain ranges stretch off into the gray distance as far as the eye can see; there is not a human sign or sound, only a faint desert breeze stirring the blossoms of brittlebush. We all should be so lucky.

On the eve of March 16, I journeyed to the edge of this desert place. March 16 is my Day of the Dead—the anniversary of the Mỹ Lai massacre in Vietnam in 1968. It was also my last day in the field in Vietnam. They choppered me east out of Bato that morning. Thirty kilometers downstream, toward the coast, we got shot at. It was no big deal, as we got shot at in helicopters all the time; but I looked down and recognized the area and the little hamlet of Mỹ Lai. I had been there earlier on the ground. At that time, I didn't know that American soldiers were systematically murdering five hundred unarmed Vietnamese civilians. It was almost a year before I saw the photos in *Life* magazine. They changed my life. From that moment on, I quite irrationally owned that problem.

March 16 was also the date in 1989 that three friends and I buried Ed Abbey here, in accordance with his last wishes. Though he died on March 14, it took a couple of days to sneak into the wilderness and find a suitable gravesite.

This March 16, I had traveled out here alone to Abbey's grave, bearing little gifts, including a bottle of mescal and a bowl of *pozole verde* I had made myself. I sat quietly on the black volcanic rocks listening to the desert silence, pouring mescal over the grave and down my throat until the moon came up an hour or so before midnight. Suddenly I heard a commotion to the south, the roar of basaltic scree thundering down the slope opposite me. A large solitary animal was headed my way.

I got the hell out of there.

Two days later I told my story of the desert bighorn ram I heard but never saw to my poet friend Jim Harrison.

"Well, Doug," Jim said, "maybe it was old Ed."

WHY I DON'T
TROPHY HUNT

About forty years ago, my friend Edward Abbey gave me a National Rifle Association (NRA) sticker to paste in the back window of my pickup. After all, he'd been an NRA member for years and we both were hunters who supported gun rights and owned firearms.

I never got around to putting on that sticker. In the decades between then and now, Ed's and my attitude toward guns didn't change much. My feelings about the NRA, however, have chilled considerably.

Increasingly, the NRA has become the big boy who thinks he can run over anyone and dominate partisan issues—they are widely criticized by environmentalists and Democrats as bullies. And the issues are no longer just those of the Second Amendment, though gun rights remain a primary test of political loyalty. An opinion piece ran in the *New York Times* that accused the NRA of now focusing on immigration, race, and health care.

The NRA is also actively trying to influence wildlife and wilderness issues, which I care about intensely. The NRA, welded at the hip to Safari Club International (SCI, a privileged group of mostly wealthy hunters dedicated to killing large and rare animals), backed a successful bill to permit extreme methods of killing wolves and grizzlies on national wildlife refuges in Alaska, including gunning down animals from planes and the slaughtering of wolf pups and bear cubs in their dens.

These two lobbying groups oppose protections for the severely endangered California condors, which biologists believe are sickened and killed by lead bullet fragments left in the hunter-felled game animals that are left for scavenging birds to feed on. The NRA and SCI pooh-poohed the notion that ingesting lead fragments harmed condors and claimed instead that their human members "will be impaired if they are no longer able to shoot lead bullets."

Similarly, the NRA and SCI recently supported a controversial trophy hunt for elephants in Zimbabwe, coinciding with the Trump administration's decision to overturn an Obama-era ban on elephant trophies. Managed trophy hunting "would not have an adverse effect on the species," the groups said, "but can further efforts to conserve the species in the wild." The US Fish and Wildlife Service's decision to allow the import of elephant trophies was praised by both groups, but drew harsh criticism from wildlife-rights advocates from all sides of the political spectrum.

———

It was no surprise when the NRA and SCI asked to intervene in a lawsuit over the fate of Yellowstone National Park's grizzly

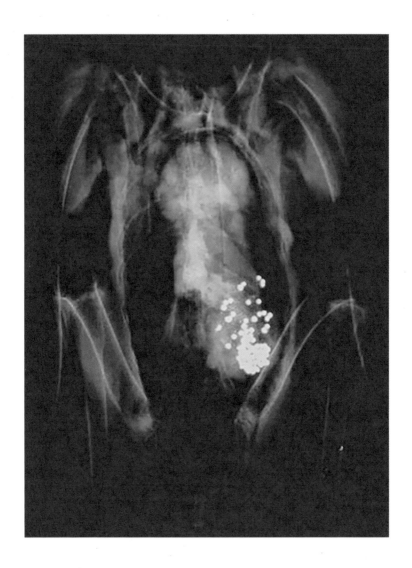

The concentrated effects of lead shot,
ingested from scavenged prey that has
been killed and left by humans, leads to
death for the bird. COURTESY OF US
GEOLOGICAL SURVEY

bear population—an issue close to my heart as well as my home. Their intent is to support the federal decision to remove the bears' Endangered Species Act protections and allow trophy hunting of Yellowstone's grizzlies.

Five NRA and SCI members said, in affidavits submitted by their attorneys, that hunting grizzlies would help the region's economy, allow states to better manage the animals, and improve public safety. These five outfitters and big-game hunters claim their interests would be harmed if they could not have the opportunity to hunt Yellowstone's grizzlies.

But the core argument is public safety: that hunting bears will make people safer by instilling in grizzlies a fear of humans. These groups claim that Yellowstone's grizzlies have become too aggressive, and that the fear of people they would develop by being hunted would make the bears shy and more subordinate, thus benefiting public safety. The unexamined assumption is that bears learn from being shot at.

The success of the NRA and SCI's argument will depend on what the judges make of the scientific plausibility of the "shy" bear theory, and the bear-expertise credibility of the five witnesses who filed declarations.

I strongly disagree with the NRA and SCI's contention that there is any credible evidence whatsoever that hunting makes grizzlies shy, wary of humans, and therefore less aggressive and safer around humans.

And there is legitimate doubt that grizzly hunting around Yellowstone is, in truth, good for the economy, and that state management is more effective than federal oversight when it comes to endangered species like the grizzly bear.

Finally, I question the grizzly-expertise of the five men who submitted affidavits to the court. The shy-bear argument, which I've been hearing in Montana bars for fifty years, is good-old-boy folklore. These men are no doubt competent backcountry professionals, but I do not believe that trophy hunting—especially the guided type, characteristic of Safari Club hunting—makes anyone an "expert" on grizzly bears. My own encounters with wild bears have made me believe that, in fact, the opposite is true: The key to safely dealing with wild grizzlies is behaving nonaggressively.

Independent biologists have reviewed the evidence and found no empirical support for the shy-bear theory. There is no evidence that a sport hunt instills fear in grizzlies, nor has research been conducted on grizzly bear hunting.

What most bear experts agree on is that American brown bears are genetically inclined to deal aggressively with perceived threats; this is evolved behavior, presumably learned on the treeless periglacial environment of the Arctic during the late Pleistocene, by mothers defending their cubs from many larger, now-extinct predators.

The NRA and SCI's theory that hunting—as a perceived threat—instills fear in bears is false. My own fifty years of experience with Yellowstone's wild grizzlies supports this position. Before 1968, I didn't know squat about grizzly bears, despite having spent a summer in Alaska. Fresh home from two tours as a Green Beret medic in Vietnam, I had gone to Yellowstone to camp and heal from a malaria attack. There, quite accidentally, I ran into a whole bunch of bears.

Here is one of my earliest encounters, from the preface of *Grizzly Years*:

"The big bear stopped thirty feet in front of me. I slowly worked my hand into my bag and gradually pulled out the Magnum. I peered down the gun barrel into the dull red eyes of the huge grizzly. He gnashed his jaws and lowered his ears. The hair on his hump stood up. We stared at each other for what might have been seconds but felt like hours. I knew that I was not going to pull the trigger. My shooting days were over. I lowered the pistol. The giant bear flicked his ears and looked off to the side. I took a step backward and turned my head toward the trees. I felt something pass between us. The grizzly slowly turned away from me with grace and dignity, and swung into the timber at the end of the meadow. I caught myself breathing heavily again, the flush of blood hot on my face. I felt my life had been touched by enormous power and mystery."

That was the last time I carried a firearm into grizzly country. I found you don't need them. I believe to this day that in bear habitat, a gun will get you into more trouble than it will get you out of.

But inexperience continued to land me in the briar patch. In my early years, I got too close to grizzlies, over a hundred encounters where the bear noticed me. That was too close in my book, as my intent was to not have the bears know I was around. When that happened, I stood my ground and the grizzlies usually—but not always—ran away.

Far more dangerously, grizzlies charged me a couple dozen times. About half of them were serious encounters: mothers with cubs or yearlings, often from nearby daybeds where they were sleeping during the middle of the day. This is the source of almost all human mauling by bears (carcasses are also dangerous): attacks by mothers near or on daybeds when humans get too close and carelessly invade the space the bear feels she needs for her cub's safety.

The sow only cares for her cub's safety. As long as you are perceived to be a threat, she will continue to charge; and if you do anything stupid, like run or try to climb a tree, she may start chewing on you. If you fight back, the mother griz will keep attacking you until you are no longer seen as a threat to her young. You could die.

The advice to "play dead" during a grizzly attack is sound. Many a victim of a mauling saved his or her life by ceasing to resist the attack, by relaxing. Tough advice, but it works.

More than a dozen different sow grizzlies have aggressively charged me. None completed her charge; no wild bear has
ever touched me. A few mother grizzlies started the charge, then
quickly veered off and ran away without breaking stride. More
often, charging bears came directly at me, and then skidded to a
stop. One sow grizzly stopped so close (probably six feet away)
she appeared to lean forward and sniff my pant leg.

During the course of all these grizzly charges, my behavior
was as nonaggressive as possible: I stood my ground without
moving a muscle or blinking an eye and looked off to the side (a
head-on orientation can be perceived as confrontational). I also
held my arms out, to make myself look bigger, and talked softly
to the bear. I hoped to present no threat whatsoever to her cubs.
It's worked every time—so far.

My most recent encounter with a mother grizzly was last
June, when my daughter and I were sheltering behind a car-sized
glacial erratic on a high mesa in Yellowstone. It was our last hike
together before I walked her down the aisle later that summer.
It was a blustery, windy day; we couldn't hear a thing. All of a
sudden, the look on my daughter's face changed and I followed
her gaze. There, some fifty feet away, a mother grizzly and her
yearling cub were coming over the top of the hillside.

We all saw each other at the same time. The mother bear
quickly reared onto her hind legs, smacked her lips, slobbered,
and looked all around. This was typical behavior for a startled
mother grizzly. I whispered to Laurel, "Don't move," and we
didn't move an inch. After several minutes, the bear calmed
down. Then, the bears slowly walked past us and sat down on
the edge of a cliff thirty feet away, where the mother began nurs-
ing the cub. This went on for about five minutes. Afterward, the
sow grizzly appeared to graze (it could have been displacement
behavior, where the nervous mom just pretended to feed) along
the lip of the cliff and the cub started to approach us, not unlike

a curious puppy. It came way too close, maybe within fifteen to twenty feet. I stopped his advance by flipping my palm, a gesture I made up in the moment, not knowing if it would work. Laurel quietly recorded a short piece of video on her phone. In the far distance, I could hear the bellows and roars of a mating pair of grizzlies far below. I think the female in front of us had retreated to this high ground to keep her cub away from aggressive male bears, who sometimes kill cubs.

This moment was saturated with wild trust, and sharing it with Laurel etched it forever in my memory. Such intimate encounters with grizzlies are rare with inland bears, like the ones in Glacier and Yellowstone Parks, but it does happen along salmon streams in places like Alaska and British Columbia. On the Nakina River in British Columbia, a mother grizzly once left her three cubs sitting next to me on the bank while she went fishing, caught a salmon, and brought it back to her waiting cubs. Biologist Larry Aumiller recorded this behavior dozens of times at the falls on the McNeil River in Alaska. So did Timothy Treadwell in Katmai on the Alaskan coast years before he made a mistake and was killed and eaten by bears. The popular thinking on this is that bear mothers trust humans because male grizzlies tend to avoid us.

I've had one experience with a service dog that I familiarized as a puppy with grizzly bear scat to get him comfortable with the scent. The idea was that we'd walk into the wind and he would alert us by vigorously wiggling his nose, then sit quietly and wait while I dealt with the bear. He passed his field test with flying colors, meeting a mother grizzly and her yearling cub near Glacier Park. I'm not looking to repeat this experiment; his younger collie brother would have gotten us killed.

This spectrum of grizzly behavior hints at a deeper social structure than bears have previously been given credit for. All wild bears in a region appear to know each other and where they rank in a larger social hierarchy. Wild grizzlies are capable of responding to nonaggressive human behavior in surprising ways and we need to give them a chance to do that. The simplistic notion that hunting and shooting grizzlies makes the bears fear humans is flat wrong.

———

There are a number of economic studies analyzing tourism in and around Yellowstone, revealing who spends what and why. The National Park Service informs us through its surveys that most Yellowstone visitors list viewing wildlife, especially grizzlies and wolves, as the primary reason for their visits. Mountain West News reported in August 2017, "Yellowstone Park tourists spent an estimated $680 million in gateway communities in Montana and Wyoming (last year)."

By contrast, proposed resident grizzly bear–hunting licenses in Wyoming would cost $600 in-state and $6,000 for out-of-staters per season. It doesn't sound like much of a comparison, except for the small consolation that trophy-bear hunters, like Safari Club members, tend to be well heeled and book the most expensive lodges.

The NRA and SCI's argument that the states of Wyoming, Montana, and Idaho are better fit than the feds to manage trophy animals is disingenuous. It has nothing to do with wildlife management competency, and everything to do with their larger political agenda.

The first objective of these two trophy-hunting groups is to kill grizzlies, and the states—Wyoming and Montana—will help them achieve this goal in record time. My specific distrust of turning brown bear management over to the states arises from how notoriously slow the departments have been to investigate and prosecute obvious cases of poaching. They are protecting illegal killers who, if caught, claim they felt threatened in some

Trophies adorn an exercise room.
DAVID CHANCELLOR

way—the "self-defense" argument. Typically, they say the bear reared, or looked at them in the wrong way, and they had to kill it. Even the wardens know this is a bald-faced lie—a rearing grizzly is the opposite of a threat. But subsequent prosecution is lax or nonexistent. To justify this nonenforcement, the state game managers say that if they prosecute poaching too aggressively, their sources of information about bear-mortality reporting will dry up. If delisting had survived its legal challenges and a hunting season was opened, illegal killing of grizzlies would have become much easier and would have loomed as the primary threat to Yellowstone's entire bear population.

Far more transparent and important, I think, is the issue of public lands. I believe these national groups have become involved with the fate of grizzlies in order to serve a broader agenda: converting public land to private ownership. To put it bluntly, stealing the land that belongs to all Americans and delivering it to the private sector for financial exploitation. They would auction off the vast wildlands of the Bureau of Land Management, national forests, and wildlife refuges, and try to open national monuments and even the national parks to resource extraction, like mining, drilling, and logging.

This so-called states' rights movement threatens all public lands. It's not just the Yellowstone ecosystem and Bears Ears National Monument that are imperiled, but also the underlying philosophy that made these places possible in the first place. The Wilderness Act, Endangered Species Act, and Antiquities Act are all under siege. The NRA and SCI agendas on wildlife and wilderness issues are, at their core, driven by the desire to dismantle our wild heritage.

In the early 1980s, I served as an expert witness on grizzly bears for Glacier National Park in federal court. The judge asked me and the other expert witness how many grizzlies (defined as different bears per day) we had seen in our lives, and because I had watched grizzly bears at Yellowstone's garbage dumps and at salmon streams as well as in berry patches and meadows, my answer was over a thousand. Does that make me an expert? Maybe for the purposes of that particular court, but otherwise I have my doubts. What teaches a person the most about grizzly behavior? Watching wild bears go about their natural business, without disturbing the animal's activity. Nature is a great classroom. Salmon streams are good, but you can also learn a great deal by watching bears far from humans in meadows and berry patches.

I've spent time with Yellowstone's grizzlies each year for the past five decades, beginning in 1968. The first fifteen years were the most intense. During that time I filmed bears full-time in the Yellowstone and Glacier National Park ecosystems. Typically, I'd spend the first six weeks of spring in Yellowstone, and then come back for October. The rest of the season, I filmed in Glacier and worked seasonal jobs for the Park Service.

Much of the time, I worked alone, lugging my heavy 16mm camera gear around in a backpack, camping in the backcountry for a couple of weeks at a time.

The goal was to film wild grizzlies close up, but not so close that the bears would be spooked by the camera noise; I wanted to capture natural grizzly behavior without the bears becoming aware of my presence. Of course, I didn't always succeed.

My strategy for finding grizzlies in Yellowstone was split between two general approaches: I could go out into good spring habitat, find a set of fresh bear tracks, and follow them to where the grizzly was feeding. Sometimes, this took several days of tracking to catch up with the bear. Compared with today, grizzlies were scarce in Yellowstone during the 1970s.

The other, more efficient strategy was to set up on a hill or promontory where bears were likely to come by, and then just wait. It helped if there was a winter-killed elk or bison carcass nearby.

Using these methods, spread over three decades, I managed to sneak up on at least two hundred unsuspecting grizzlies in and around Yellowstone and Glacier parks, to distances within about one hundred yards. Most of those approached were captured on film, which is now archived at Texas Tech University.

From my experience, I don't think dispatching brown bears with a weapon capable of bringing down a B-52 would be very challenging. I could have shot any of those bears; grizzlies are easy to hunt. Easy, say, compared to black bears, who are spooky forest creatures and a test for a fair-chase (no baits or dogs) hunter. Grizzlies, by contrast, are open-country animals and their dominance at the top of the food chain means they don't automatically run away.

But does tracking down a wild griz with a camera equate with trophy hunting? Absolutely not, as any Safari Club International member would point out. Why? I didn't pull the trigger. There was no kill. Without the kill, there is no "authentic hunt."

Here is a crucial distinction between trophy hunters and me: I don't hunt predators. I wouldn't shoot a bear for a cool million.

How do you justify killing an innocent animal of exceptional carriage that you don't intend to eat and that poses no threat to you? A few trophy hunters try to answer this question, but most see no problem; they kill the big grizzly or the lion with a huge mane because they can. There are arguments: Money for permits and licenses can be spent on conservation. You may trophy hunt because it runs in the family. Or because male archetypes like Teddy Roosevelt or Ernest Hemingway did it.

When we think of trophy hunters, the photo of Donald Trump Jr. holding a freshly severed elephant tail may come to mind, but I recognize a few other types, often deeply skilled in the ways of the wild and dedicated to a fair chase. The ones I know tend to be bow hunters. These people are probably the exception: They know why they are out there and are grounded in their own ethic.

Of those Safari Club members who have shown any curiosity at all about their deadly sport, it's probably fair to say the bulk have drawn their killer philosophies from mid-twentieth-century sources, especially a little book called *Meditations on Hunting*, written in 1942 by elite Spanish philosopher José Ortega y Gasset. This book is quoted very often in the literature of trophy hunting.

Ortega tells us death is essential because without it there is no authentic hunting. In short, one does not hunt in order to kill; on the contrary, one kills in order to have hunted.

The author Tovar Cerulli's critique of Ortega is valuable, "the animal's death is a 'sign' that the hunt was 'authentic' and 'real.'" This European view of killing and the hunt owes nothing to the roughly 315,000 years of *Homo sapiens'* wildlife experience: After all, we evolved chasing animals in the Pleistocene, in habitats whose remnants we now call the wilderness.

Throw in some colonial dominance over the beasts, a little Hemingway, and you find a tremendous amount of masculine bullshit in consideration of what constitutes an authentic experience in outdoor blood sports. Cerulli continues, "Ortega celebrates the 'exemplary moral spirit of the sporting hunter' who hunts for 'diversion.' He looks down on the 'utilitarian' hunter, like 'Paleolithic man and ... the poacher of any epoch,' [or individuals like me] who hunt for food."

For the record, I do hunt, mostly game birds and the occasional deer. In my youth, I shot a porcupine and a raccoon; I was the only kid in high school eating raccoon and porcupine sandwiches. I eat what I kill, and I have a bunch of guns. I don't hunt predators or trophy-sized animals (for practical and culinary reasons).

Despite a few female members, groups like the Safari Club are solidly rooted in the masculine institutions of patriarchy and clanship. Within the fraternal organization, intense competition abounds. If your buddy bags a huge kudu or leopard, you'd better get a bigger one. This deadly rivalry about who gets the best trophy is regarded as either the purest form of sport, as seen by the Safari Club, or one of the worst contests in our society, as viewed by people like me.

The time for these ceremonial executions is over. We lost our authenticity somewhere in the colonial past. These often endangered and expendable trophy creatures could use a break from recreational killing. We don't need a Yellowstone grizzly hunt. This argument would be a silly one if the consequences were not so deadly.

The man holding the cut-off elephant tail may take exception, but we are many decades down the road from the faded photos of Teddy Roosevelt's rhino in 1909 or Hemingway's lion photo in 1934—archetypical images of man's dominion over the animals. Our view of seeing ourselves as separate from nature is the path that has delivered us to today's peril. The year 2021 finds us in the middle of the sixth great extinction, largely driven by climate change and entirely caused by human activity.

The fact that we are still debating trophy hunting shows us how far we still need to go to stop the plunder of the Earth. The first critters to go in a great extinction tend to be the big ones, especially the large and rare mammals favored by trophy hunters, like the rhino whose disappearance is being driven by poaching. Will human civilization escape the planet's baking heat? This endangered species list does not exclude two-legged primates; the hot winds of climate change are coming for us all.

Teddy Roosevelt with his African rhino
in Kenya, 1909. KERMIT ROOSEVELT/
SCIENCE SOURCE

SHEEPHERDER STEW FOR ABBEY

On March 14, 1989, desert anarchist and writer Edward Abbey died. I attended his death, administering medicine, injections, and other hopeless remedies that last night. Two days later, three friends and I buried him in a desert grave.

Ed's passing was a significant landmark in my life, a winter count. Abbey's death was no surprise, as the doctors had misdiagnosed his portal hypertension as cancer of the head of the pancreas. Ed was repeatedly told he had only a year or less to live over a five-year period. He bore this misinformation with great dignity.

Since Abbey had some time to think about it, he scribbled down some notes about his death and burial. This is what we had to work with:

Funeral Instructions
Ceremony? Gunfire and a little music please,

Previous spread: The Granite Window
in the Cabeza Prieta National Wildlife
Refuge, Arizona. DAVID MUENCH

Above: Ed Abbey plugs an intruder
outside his writer's shack in the Tucson
Mountains, Arizona. TERRENCE MOORE

*maybe a few readings from Thoreau, Whitman,
Twain, Jeffers, and/or Abbey, etc.; that should
be sufficient. No speeches desired, though the de-
ceased will not interfere if someone feels the urge.
But keep it all simple and brief.*

*A wake! More music, lots of gay and lively music—
bagpipes! Drums and flutes! Jigs, reels, country
swing, and polkas. I want dancing! And a flood of
beer and booze! A bonfire! And lots of food—meat!
Jerky and sheepherder stew. Gifts for all my friends
and all who come—books, record albums, curios,
and keepsakes. No formal mourning, please—lots
of singing, dancing, talking, hollering, laughing,
and lovemaking instead. Some gunfire! Doug and
his guns.*

———

It wasn't an easy task to bury Ed; it took a couple of days to find
the precise wilderness gravesite and there was plenty of squabbling among the team along the way. Three close friends shared
the duties with me: Ed's father-in-law, Clarke's brother-in-law,
and my friend Jack Loeffler. Not all of us were comfortable
with this forbidden labor; this was illegal transport of an un-
embalmed body, without permits, and internment in prohibited
soil. Steve, Clarke's brother-in-law, became my instant friend
and guided me through my own hard landing following our
planting old Ed in his final home—a mixture of grief, flashbacks,
and fatigue.

I was exhausted when I got back to Tucson. Clarke (Ed's wife)
had scheduled a wake for Ed in just three days. My job would
be cooking the sheepherder stew and smoking the jerky—plenty
of work.

The event would be a public wake for his friends and fans. I owed this to Abbey's family and followers. It was my notion of service. Food had to be prepared. I needed to get my hands on some meat. What came to mind was a cow.

An obscene picture had recently been published of sixteen severed mountain lion heads stacked in a pyramid against a tree. Government animal control agents had slaughtered them at the request of a single cattle rancher on US Forest Service land, so I had a steer from that particular ranch in mind—a very minor gesture of payback.

I had always been aware that I needed physical risk in my life. I didn't know why—it was something I'd never analyzed. Maybe I required just a little danger—a little hazard fix—to imagine myself a tiny bit brave and competent. Sometimes it helped if the risk was slightly illegal, like a modern-day equivalent of a Crow stealing a Cheyenne pony. I had a vague notion that these acts reaffirmed me among my people, men and women who kept the faith alive by taking care of one another and fighting to protect the wild homeland—Abbey's people.

Now with Ed in his grave, the hour had arrived for me to seriously reconsider my unsolicited part-time career as an environmental outlaw. After all, I had children of my own, a family to support. Even the most righteous monkey wrenching constituted illegal acts that could land me in the slammer. I not only knew right from wrong; I knew what was legal and what was not. But I still had Ed-related duties: one foray with the gang remained.

It now happened that these circumstances—Ed's death, the mountain lion heads, the need to execute a little illegal act in reaffirmation of Abbey's honor, and getting the meat essential for Ed's wake—came into alignment.

After atrocities as immoral as body counts, the corrupt yet legal act of killing large numbers of Arizona's mountain lions and black bears on a single ranch running cattle on leases that were 98 percent on public land was unacceptable in my world.

My plan was to go out to the lion- and bear-killer's lease on the national forest and poach one of his slow elk for Ed's wake (Native Americans, especially the bison-hunting Plains Nations, called White Man's cattle "slow elk"). These Natives noted that the "spotted buffalo," or range cow—in comparison with a wild animal—was markedly dim-witted and slow of foot. I had discussed lion payback with Abbey months before his death. Ed approved of the general plan. Of course, I didn't anticipate Abbey being dead before the payback. Now, justice would be another spice for the stew.

Abbey deserved an honoring. The least I could do would be to execute his "Funeral Instructions" with a flourish.

Poaching slow elk is, simply put, cattle rustling, punishable everywhere in these parts and throughout the West by imprisonment, hanging, or something in-between.

The next morning, I went hunting with two pals. We pored over topographic, land-ownership, and national forest maps. Our approach to the grazing lease would be from the wilderness.

The pickup truck ground up steep primitive roads and then tracks. When the tracks petered out altogether we left the truck, but before we left it, I replaced the license plates with ones registered to Ed, who had no more need of them.

Dressed in camouflage, carrying binoculars and .22 rifles, and wearing sidearms, we picked our way through the agave and prickly pear. My two companions were known and dedicated Earth First! activists. One of them was an accomplished woodsman capable of talking to ravens and calling in mountain lions by clacking together two sets of deer antlers. The country seemed overgrazed. This cattle-grazing lease was, in fact, a perfect illustration of everything gone wrong with public land in the West—national forest land—where unbelievable numbers of coyotes, eagles, the last recorded Arizona wolf, skunks, badgers, coatimundis, ringtail cats, bobcats, mountain lions, and black bears have died unspeakable deaths in the jaws of the rancher's steel traps and by poison at the hands of the tax-payer-supported Animal Damage Control agents of the federal Department of Agriculture. This trapping was legal and intended to protect the rancher's cattle; our hunt was quite illegal and intended to harm the rancher's cattle.

At dusk we startled an ocelot, a very rare cat this far north. We made a cold camp and turned in. During the night, curious and bold ringtails checked us out.

The next morning, we heard, spotted, and began stalking wild range cattle, man-shy animals that ran off. After two hours, we finally crept up on a thousand-pound cow and shot it cleanly between the eyes. This was a slow-elk hunt, and humane execution was mandatory. Ed Abbey had specified: "no gut shooting."

In this rugged wild country, the beast was too big to move. We peeled the hide back with our knives on the spot and went to work. We cut out a hundred pounds of tenderloin and sirloin with our skinning knives, leaving nine hundred pounds for the bears, skunks, coatis, cats, coyotes, and ravens. The meat we took would go into beef jerky and sheepherder stew for Abbey's wake.

———

At my home in Tucson, I cleared out friends who were camped in my backyard waiting for Abbey's wake. Sometimes I forgot that Ed had also been a man of considerable fame. I told these tribesmen to please go up to Cerro Prieto—the place I had intended to take Ed to die Sunday morning when we ran out of time—and see the beautiful ironwood desert, visit the ancient petroglyphs, and camp there for the night. I needed some space, a bit of solitude, and lots of time.

Despite Abbey's request for a joyful wake, I really didn't expect people to be in a festive mood or to be particularly appreciative of exquisite food. This was OK. I was cooking for Ed now and I didn't especially care about the mourners. I wanted to serve up a great sheepherder stew and the best goddamned jerky anyone ever tasted. A little cholesterol can't hurt you when you're dead.

I transferred the plastic bags of sirloin and tenderloin to a big freezer, wanting to put a hard chill on the poached meat, just a touch of frost to make cutting the slow elk into hunks and cubes easy. Meanwhile, I got out my best steel and hard Arkansas sharpening stone. I took a folding chair and put it out in the sun next to a big mesquite log. The backyard birds were active. I rummaged through my three backpacks and the pickup and found all my favorite knives; I laid these out on the log in preparation for sharpening.

There was my old Bowie knife that was given to me by my first love on my birthday, and Hayduke's knife, the Buck "Especial," which Ed Abbey bought while he was writing *The Monkey Wrench Gang* and later gave to me. There were whittling knives from my two departed grandfathers, and from my dad, my Special Forces knife engraved with the insignia of the 5th Special Forces Group (Airborne)-Vietnam. And an old sheath knife I had last used a decade and a half ago to open a can of dog food for my beloved collie dog Larry, now gone, the animal that had gone along with Abbey and me to the Cabeza Prieta in 1974 (*The Monkey Wrench Gang* year) and on many other wilderness journeys.

I thought of the places I had carried these knives, the fight in which I almost used the canned-dog-food knife, the people who had been with me—those places and times charted by these blades of steel. They had traveled the American West from the jungles of Mexico to the Arctic Sea, cleaned trout and salmon across the Arctic, down the Pacific Northwest, and in every state in the Rockies all the way down to Mexico, high up above Basa-seachic Falls in the Sierra Madre in Sonora.

The Bowie knife and Especial had traveled with Abbey and me on our camping and backpacking trips throughout southern Utah, places that bear the names: the Kaiparowits, Willow, Fortymile, Coyote Gulch, Escalante, Comb Ridge, Mill Creek, Cathedral Valley, Lavender, and Salt Creek Canyon. I had also carried them on other trips, outings, and nefarious night jobs along the freeways and housing developments of the American Southwest.

I started on the old Bowie knife, which was made of soft Solingen steel and was easy to put an edge on. It had been used recently, near Ed's house on the side walls of the giant tires on the land developer's earthmoving equipment parked near Abbey's backyard. A few strokes sufficed to put an edge back on. The Especial was still pretty sharp; I drew the blade across the Arkansas stone, taking thin, little slices, always at a constant angle, alternating sides until the knife took the hair off my wrist.

The Special Forces Ka-Bar from Vietnam was more a souvenir of war than a functional tool. It was so hard you could cut wire or even nails with it; the downside was it took forever to resharpen. Besides, the hard temper rendered the material a bit brittle, and I had broken off the tip prying open a large oyster on a Brewster beach in Cape Cod during a winter of despair when I had followed a nurse back East. The dog-food-can knife was nicked and blunted from opening numerous cans of Alpo and needed serious attention.

I went inside and grabbed a bottle of Pacifico beer and squeezed a lime into it. Coming out, I scattered a flock of fifteen Inca doves. Back in the sunlight, I sat down and pulled out the damaged knife. Drawing the blade down one side of the steel, then the other, I worked at it for ten minutes. One of the nicks was big and caught each time I drew it across the steel. I thought about taking a file to it, then remembered the can of dog food that had caused the nick, a can opened near the Needles Overlook southwest of the La Sals during the late autumn of 1974. I had been camping out with my loyal collie at my side, reading *The Monkey Wrench Gang* manuscript, which Abbey asked me to read and "do the technical editing." I camped on the rim west of Horsehead Rock for two days, looking out into space toward Rustler Canyon in the northern Needles District of Canyonlands National Park, while sitting on the rim reading Doc's and Hayduke's adventures.

I had held it together throughout the weeks of Ed's last illness, his death, and burial. It had been all business and there had been no time for grief. Now, however, remembering the collie and the can of Alpo, a shudder ran up my spine and I began to sob and shake. I looked around the yard to see if anyone was about. Done with the knives, I went inside and splashed water on my face. This was not seemly behavior for a wake.

I brought in the frosted meat from the freezer, laid it on the chopping block, and put on Bruckner's Symphony no. 4, *Romantic*, which I didn't get to play much because Lisa, my wife, couldn't stand it. Nearly everyone I knew disliked this composer except Ed and me. The music billowed and strained. I sliced the tenderloin with the grain, cutting it into long strips about an inch in diameter, and repeated the process with the big hunks of top sirloin, setting aside a half-dozen pounds of strips for jerky.

I worked slowly, enjoying the repetitive movements, cubing and slicing—cutting the meat was a simple pleasure. Bruckner finished with a flourish and I replaced him with Sibelius, another Romantic composer Ed was fond of. I diced five pounds of mesquite bacon and dumped it into rapidly boiling water in the cast-iron Dutch oven that the Abbeys had given me as a wedding gift. After ten minutes, I poured the contents into a colander, scrubbed the pot, and then returned the parboiled bacon along with several big dollops of olive oil.

Despite Ed's affection for Sibelius, I interrupted his *Finlandia* for a Mozart violin and viola concerto. I turned up the heat under the Dutch oven until the mixture of bacon grease and olive oil began to smoke a bit. I dropped the cubes of beef into the hot oil and seared them on all sides. As the meat browned, I lifted out the cubes with a slotted spoon I had inadvertently liberated from Huckleberry Lookout in Glacier National Park, where Ed and I had both worked as fire lookouts during the 1970s. I added more cubes of beef, a dozen or so at a time. With over fifty pounds of meat, this took a while.

When all the meat was seared, I browned two bunches of carrots and a couple hundred small white onions in what was left of the same batch of oil. When I was finished with the vegetables, I tossed out the oil. By now I had a mountain of meat, which I divided among four big, deep casserole dishes.

I popped the cork on one of my best bottles from my small but adequate stash of Bordeaux, a 1970 Les Forts de Latour, poured a full glass for the cook, and put on a Beethoven string quartet, Opus 132. I remembered the first time I played this late quartet for Abbey, on the rim of Escalante Canyon in 1971.

One of Ed's few literary misgivings was a passage on music in *Desert Solitaire*, during which he had dismissed Mozart while endorsing the thin-textured works of Berg, Webern, and Schoenberg. "I'd do anything to have those three pages back," Ed once told me. Abbey later came to love the perfect lightness of Mozart and the depth of the later Beethoven music, especially during the season of desert flowering and storms, or for sunsets.

I let my mind go, wallowing in memories like a warthog in mud. I found my stash of dried yellow chanterelle mushrooms, which I had picked in grizzly country, mostly Yellowstone, during the past three autumns. The association of wild mushrooms with grizzly bears, for me, was unmistakable. The other dried mushrooms, a smaller bag of big white chanterelles, had been picked with Peter Matthiessen below the "Grizzly Hilton," a range of hills that I visited each year near Glacier National Park in Montana. Of the ten or fifteen people I had taken up to the Grizzly Hilton over the past fifteen years, the only person to make the trip without seeing a grizzly was Edward Abbey. Ed went to his death without ever spotting one; he called my favorite animal "the alleged grizzly." Peter saw twenty-five.

Contrasted with other dried mushrooms, such as morels or boletus, the chanterelles from grizzly country didn't reconstitute well, though the liquid you soaked them in carried considerable flavor. One approach to a surplus of dried chanterelles was to pulverize them in a food processor. That was what I had intended for the sheepherder stew. I poured another glass of Bordeaux and punched the button.

The harsh whine and metallic grind of the processor clashed with the string quartet and abraded my nerves, and after a minute I turned it off. I dumped the dried and chopped-up mushrooms into a big stone metate used by the ancient Hohokam eight hundred years ago. My children, Laurel and Colin, and Ed's two youngest, Rebecca and Ben, found it three miles from our house. In the metate was a basaltic mano or grinding stone, from the same site.

I used the grinding stone to pulverize the dried mushrooms into chanterelle powder and tossed the browned pieces of slow elk in the mixture of flour and ground mushrooms. Meanwhile, I preheated the oven and chopped up a dozen heads of garlic. I tossed the cubes of slow elk for a few more minutes until they were coated with a light crust, and when the oven reached the right temperature, I put in the dishes of cubes.

Now I needed more cooking wine so I opened another bottle, a Château Lynch-Bages, thinking this was more than I could easily afford—I had two young children and made less than fifteen grand a year. After three glasses, I poured the entire remaining

Sus Picnic Area where the public wake for
Ed Abbey was held. Arizona. RICHARD
WALKER/CREATIVE COMMONS

contents of the Bordeaux over the works. The level of wine and stock was a bit low, so I opened a big Zinfandel and poured it in, bringing the level of wine up until it barely covered the slow elk. I turned down the oven and took a break outside, watching the high clouds prepare for sunset, and finished my wine.

My plan was to cook the meat at a simmer for a couple of hours, then finish the sheepherder stew tomorrow morning before the wake. I'd get up early and also smoke the jerky.

Meanwhile, I needed to make the marinade for the jerky. I took a gallon of unfiltered apple juice and added in a six-pack of Mexican beer—minus a can for the cook—dumped in about three cups of sugar and one of salt, and then added a few splashes of tamari sauce, a bit of Worcestershire and hot sauce, garlic, and a lot of coarse-ground black and lemon pepper. By now, I was tired.

It had been an agreeable day full of uncomplicated kitchen procedures, food preparation, and simple cooking, accompanied by fine wine and great music—the remembering of good times and friends. I slipped easily from my solitude and indulgence as Lisa pulled into the driveway with the children.

———

The next morning, I rose at daylight. I put on coffee, went into the fridge, retrieved the jerky makings, and dumped the strips of sirloin into the marinade. I stepped outside, mindlessly heading to the mailbox to get the morning newspaper. The desert sky was an unsurpassed spring blue still darkening toward turquoise in the fading marl of sunrise. Tiny trumpets of red penstemon, yellow brittlebush, and marigold blossomed along my driveway. Beyond the confines of landscape and culture, the entire Sonoran Desert pushed up flowers of every shade of color. It was a great day to be alive.

The paper had a small news piece about Edward Abbey along with a photograph of Ed I had taken fifteen years ago in the

Superstition Mountains of Arizona. I hadn't seen the photo in a long time, though it had been published hundreds of times. The first publisher of *The Monkey Wrench Gang* had used the slide as an author photo on the back cover of the jacket and had never bothered returning it to me. The article mentioned the public wake that was to be held today at the Sus Picnic Area in the west sector of Saguaro National Park.

I grabbed a section of newspaper and carried it into my backyard, startling a flock of Inca doves, several white-wings, a Gila woodpecker, curve-billed thrashers, a brown towhee, a covey of Gambel's quail, pyrrhuloxias, a handsome cardinal couple, a cottontail, and two young black-tailed jackrabbits. My new bird feeder, a birthday present from Clarke Abbey, was paying dividends. I assembled the little portable smoker. It was one of those seventeen-inch cylindrical arrangements with two racks over a pan for the marinade and another in the bottom for hot coals and wood chips. I pitched in a handful of mesquite wood chips. The smoker was cooking away at about 150 degrees Fahrenheit, good enough for a quick batch of moist jerky.

I sautéed some shallots in butter with an equivalent amount of garlic. When these were translucent, I added a bowl of fresh mushrooms and about three cups of diced green pepper. After a few minutes I added a tad of soy and a few drops of maple syrup. I dumped in the chanterelle liquid and cooked it down to the viscosity of 20-weight motor oil, thickening it just a bit with arrowroot flour. I brown-braised and parboiled the white onions in slow elk stock, and set the mushrooms and onions off to the side.

I was close to done. I took out the casserole dishes of meat and returned them to the heat, skimming off the fat one last time. I filtered the entire lot and washed out the dishes, returning the meat and adding the vegetables, and simmered it until it was time to take the jerky from the smoker and drive over the

Ed Abbey on Isla Ángel de la Guarda in the
Sea of Cortez where he went with Doug
and friends, 1977. Baja California, Mexico.
TERRENCE MOORE

little mountains behind my house into Saguaro National Park, through the lush cactus and ironwood desert to the public wake for Edward Abbey.

The back road to Sus Picnic Area wound around a granite outcrop where the Abbeys and the Peacocks routinely held cookouts and barbeques with friends. I wondered about my role in public life after Ed Abbey's death: I was already known in the wilderness movement and embodied the earthly remains of George Washington Hayduke. The cooking was service to his people. The tribulations of preparing sheepherder stew and the voluntary agonies of attending to the dying and burial struck me as some kind of penitence. Why? Could I have been a better friend, husband, or father? Abbey also struggled with balancing a love of wilderness with a love of family. I knew I had turned a corner and had work to do. Ed's passing refuted the notion that death can render a life meaningless. We would see.

MONSOON

A lifetime ago I ran into a man who told me about some ancient cave paintings in the central mountains of Baja California. This fellow, a Black guy from Louisiana, drew me a map to one of these caves on the back of a napkin. I had been stuck for a few days at a beachside hotel in La Paz at Christmastime. The cheapest place to eat well was a rib joint run by this man who was from somewhere around Baton Rouge. This guy was no longer American; he had been around awhile and had a Mexican wife and kid. Louisiana was a place he didn't care to go back to. He said this cave in a canyon near Mulegé was like nothing he had ever seen before. I decided then that I'd have to see it for myself.

I didn't get down to Baja again for another couple of years, and when I did, it was a quick, impulsive summer trip. By then, I was sort of on the lam myself, taking a cheap vacation from a malady I'd tried to flee for years only to discover I couldn't get out from under the open sky. I was vainly hoping I'd run into

Previous spread: Blasting down the
road in Baja California, Mexico.
CHRISTOPHER KIMMEL/GETTY IMAGES

something as hard as the head of a glacier or as potent as a face-off with a grizzly.

The problem seemed to be I wanted a life beyond the war zone, but not in the world I had come back to. I wanted to live in the land I remember leaving behind before Southeast Asia—the grand topography of the American West and Rocky Mountains. Returning, I found it transformed by drilling rigs, power plants belching black death, connected spiderlike by hundreds of miles of power lines, with clear-cuts and development sprawl-ing across the mountains, deserts, and plains. After Vietnam, I couldn't bear the destruction of that particular beauty.

I blasted down the searing 601 miles of pavement, only stop-ping for gas in Tijuana, with the soul of a penitent, thinking many people would consider an August trip down the peninsula a holiday in hell. The summer weather of central Baja could be hot, exceedingly hot and humid; only the monsoon softens the hammer of sun on the volcanic anvil of the Sierra de Guadalupe. These summer thunderstorms mark the renewal of life; the land is reborn and the desert year begins again. Sudden torrential rains scour the canyons and cleanse the washes, insects hatch and birds feed, and, as if by a miracle, the Earth turns green.

I parked my truck near the end of the dirt road, and hiked up the trail a mile to the mouth of the canyon. Palo blanco and paloverde trees blanketed the canyon bottom and everything was covered with green vines. The day was already hot, the mid-day sun reflecting off the sand of the arroyo, and the humidity poured off the vines and bushes. Flocks of white-winged doves startled, bursting from the thickets every minute or so. Clouds of insects and black-tailed gnatcatchers buzzed the treetops, and beyond were thousands of butterflies of every color.

I passed a deserted rancheria with goat pens fenced to giant fig trees. The canyon narrowed and the trail, now only a goat path, climbed steeply up the south side of the arroyo. I climbed up through the cliffs and broke into the open. The morning wind blowing down the canyon had died to a gentle breeze. The tops of a few thunderheads loomed above the dark peaks. The cumulus clouds were small but still building; it would be a while before any weather rolled in. Between the cliffs were sloping terraces of elephant trees and cactus; below was the inner gorge, a green jungle penetrated by an occasional fan palm.

The cave didn't look like much at first. If the trail were not there, you could have bushwhacked right on past without noticing it. The cave was upslope, at the foot of a cliff of dacite, and eighty feet deep as I later paced it. I was expecting cave paintings, but nothing prepared me for the scale or power of that scene.

Some eighty figures, life-size and bigger, mostly human but also fish and deer, were painted in red, black, white, or half red and half black across the ceiling of the cave. Fifty of these stiff, slightly bulbous human figures were painted from the front with outthrust arms like fat gingerbread men. The biggest were eight feet long and arranged in random orientations, as if floating on a windless surface like autumn leaves caught in an eddy. Some had headdresses. All the male representations had their arms outstretched, and arrows—some carefully painted to show feathers and arrowheads—impaled them all. Only the paintings of women and a crosshatched scarecrow figure—apparently one of the oldest, as evidenced by overpaintings—had been spared this symbolic fate.

I stepped outside, away from the riveting magnet of the panel of prehistoric art. Flycatchers and Say's phoebes rolled off the treetops of the canyon bottom, a churning wave of insects and birds. And now there were butterflies everywhere. A snowstorm of white and yellow butterflies filled the valley, a cloud of wings from the bottom of the arroyo to the rim and almost as wide as the canyon itself. A huge black rock sat across the canyon, partially blocking the bottom as if misplaced by some error of

A cave with prehistoric paintings in the
Sierra de Guadalupe in Baja California,
Mexico. TERRENCE MOORE

hydraulics. A mile upstream, the dark barranca forked abruptly, carving the mountain above into a somber pyramid. A thunderhead passed over the sun. Instantly, the blizzard of butterflies vanished, the insects retiring to the undersides of leaves. The birds were still noisy, and somewhere in the bottom I could hear frogs. It looked like a storm was coming my way.

I went back to the cave and looked up. A few white fish, up to six feet long, were painted over figures at the back of the cave. Outside, distant thunder reverberated down the canyon. Some of the figures were twenty feet off the ground. The Native Americans here had told the Jesuits that the painting was done by a race of giants who had died from gambling debts in which they bet their lives and lost; other giants were changed into rocks.

Beside the paintings of fish there was a single life-size deer. But the great art on the ceiling of the cave was not about life or hunting. It was an unmistakable death scene. The figures were bloated, as they would be from the desert heat, and penetrated by as many as six spears and arrows. Maybe the mural was about sorcery or war: The homicidal panorama seemed to be of a pitched battle, though the tribes in Baja were not known to wage such warfare. Something bad must have happened here.

More thunder boomed and the temperature was dropping rapidly. Wind whipped down the canyon and I felt the first sting of rain on my face. I retreated to the back of the cave and watched as the full force of the late-summer monsoon hit the valley.

Squalls of rain pelted the mouth of the cave. Beyond, I could see thin waterfalls of mud running off the rim and pouring into the gorge. I looked out through dozens of tiny rivulets draining off the lip of the cave entrance.

Within ten minutes, the rain slackened and the storm rapidly abated. I walked out to the rim and watched a hundred muddy waterfalls dwindle to drips, and at first, it was quiet. Gradually though, I heard the faint stir of insects and birds, and then a few minutes later something like the drone of a small aircraft. I couldn't quite make it out, but it was growing louder. The buzz heightened to a distant roar. I climbed down to investigate, dropping through the cliffs until I stood above the inner gorge of the canyon. Abruptly, the wind picked up, blowing cold air down the canyon.

The sudden musk of humus—the fetor of earth—impregnated the atmosphere. I experienced a second of confusion, overpowered by the earthy pungency, feeling the air might explode. Then, at the edge of the giant black rock, a wall of water burst through.

I watched the flash flood rage below me from my safe perch on the bench. A log and boulder caught in a mat of sticks alongside the big black rock, finally forcing the tangle down over the falls and into the trees below. The sound of rushing water was deafening. A shaft of sunlight pierced the clouds. Steam rose from the cliffs and ledges, and fragments of clouds hung below the rim.

I returned to the cave but did not enter. I didn't belong here. This was a place of magic and I had received my dose. The violent storm had scoured the canyon and washed away my tracks; in its destructive force resided a new beginning, the power to transform the land and all that lived in it.

It began to warm up. As I turned to leave, the butterflies started to come back out, swarms of yellow and white wings disappearing into the scudding clouds and re-emerging on the other side as a gasp of color.

HEADWATERS

The Montana summer day eased toward the coolness of evening. As the shadows crawled across the river, swarms of insects began to churn above the shaded water along the bank, spreading until the water's surface was fogged with a rolling haze of caddis and pale mayfly duns. Trout began to rise along the rocks and at the current's edge. At the edge of a deep slot along the far bank, a thirteen-inch rainbow jumped clear of the water. I grabbed my fly rod hoping to get a cast off as I floated past. But before I could strip any line off, the drift boat slammed into a rock and pivoted off toward another. I dropped the rod and picked up the oars again. Fly fishing the Big Hole River while rowing a boat solo in low water was next to impossible.

Five weeks after I buried Ed Abbey, the FBI showed up knocking on the doorstep of my home in Tucson; it was the day of the Earth First! bust. Two and a half months later it was now July 1989 and no one had seen me push off into the river.

Previous spread: The headwaters of the
Missouri River, Montana. ANDY AUSTIN

No vehicle or boat trailer remained behind to mark my departure at the launch site near Divide, Montana. My friend, the writer Jim Crumley, dropped my gear and me off below the bridge, and then towed the old boat trailer to Livingston. No one besides Crumley knew I was here, and no one knew how fast or how far I might travel downstream. I didn't know myself. Since I had no way to get off the river—no truck and trailer waiting downriver—I just had to keep moving. I had some rudimentary maps but no details showing what awaited me on the rivers below. I'd have to wing it.

The Big Hole ran another fifty miles south and east, hooking into the Beaverhead near Twin Bridges, after which it was called the Jefferson. The Jefferson meandered another hundred miles back to the northeast where it joined two other great rivers, the Gallatin and the Madison, to create the headwaters of the Missouri River. No matter how long it took—and it could take weeks—or how difficult the route, I wanted to drift downstream at least as far as the headwaters of the Missouri.

The boat I was rowing was a windfall from the breakup of my in-laws. As they were growing up, Lisa and her siblings called the plywood McKenzie-style drift boat the *Green Queen*, and the name stuck.

My biggest immediate worry was low water. Scarcely a cloud had decorated the incomparable Montana sky in a month of hot days that would only get hotter. This was the second year of a major drought in the West. My old drift boat was already scraping over rocks in the riffles and shallows of the tailouts. As I progressed downstream, tributaries and springs dumped more water into the river, and it would theoretically grow deeper, heavier in flow, and more powerful. The problem was that ranchers diverted an incredible amount of water out of the river to irrigate alfalfa fields to feed their cattle. The agricultural drain more than compensated for the natural feed of the creeks and springs.

Diversion dams blocked the river in numerous places to channel the flow into irrigation canals. These little dams, usually constructed of old concrete slabs, were the biggest and probably the only obstacle to floating all the way down to the Missouri, where you hit the really big dams. I didn't know how many little dams there were or exactly how to get around or through them. Since the boat was too heavy to carry, I'd either have to line through the dams or push the three hundred–pound craft along the bank on rollers made out of logs and poles. It didn't actually matter, as I had no choice but to keep going; I'd figure it out as I moved downstream.

I maneuvered the wooden dory around bucket-sized boulders into the main tongue of the river. The boat scraped the bottom in the shallows at the head of the run and again just at the tail-out of the little rapids. Trout were rising with regularity, but I kept at the oars for another half hour; I wanted to get a few miles away from the bridge and out of sight of any road or ranch by dark. I still had to find a hidden campsite and figured I had only enough light to see and avoid hitting the rocks for another forty-five minutes.

The river bent to the left and disappeared against the dim light of a bank of cliffs about two hundred yards downstream. On the right was a strip of cottonwoods separating the river from a fallow pasture beyond. I figured that was far enough, and I pulled hard on the wooden oars and drove the bow of the heavy boat up onto the muddy bank next to the big trees. I'd make camp here.

Mosquitoes buzzed around my ears. I slapped on a splash of Vietnam War–surplus "jungle juice" on my neck, face, and balding head. The bugs would disappear as the temperature dropped after dark. I'd handle the tent then; putting it up in the darkness was no big deal. Now I wanted to fish.

About fishing: I was raised fly fishing by my dad, uncles, and grandfather on trout streams in Michigan. These days, in

Montana, I still fish. But I'm not exactly a recreational fisher-man. I grew up catching fish for dinner, and that peasant utility clashes with the sportsman's approach to catch-and-release fly fishing. But here I was stuck on this river for perhaps weeks with way too much time to think. I needed some diversion, and this was one of the best trout streams in the country.

I waded out into the cool river in long pants and rubber san-dals. A mini-flashlight hung around my neck from a nylon cord and I held it in my mouth as I tied on a size 16 red quill fly with the aid of Kmart reading glasses; it was all I could do to find the eye of the tiny hook—the limitations of middle-aged eyesight.

Trout were rising everywhere. The ones close to me that I could see in the fading light were small, but I could hear some bigger splashes toward the head of the run. I waded upstream, casting across and slightly upriver to rising fish along the way.

The truth was I hadn't seen a night like this in a long time; sometime after Vietnam I had lost, without ever having been aware of the precise moment, the pleasure of night fishing. This evening was like my boyhood in northern Michigan. I remem-bered three nights during the 1950s on the Pine River at my grandfather's cabin when fish—hundreds more than you could imagine living there—fed voraciously on the surface, rising to big caddis flies, mayflies, and crane flies. I remember standing on the bridge by Grandpa's cabin in the dark, the moon not yet up, and hearing several dozen splashes every minute, including lunker browns by Michigan standards of three or more pounds. Forty years later, standing on the edge of the current of the Big Hole River, I felt all the old magic again.

Thirty feet below the top of the run I stopped. The main slick of rapids was another twenty feet out.

I cast near the bank to measure the line, then dropped the fly a couple of feet upstream of the biggest feeding fish and a foot off to the side. The line had enough slack in it to drift flawlessly over the trout. Nothing doing. A second later the big fish rose again. I tried a second cast, but the fly dragged just at the point of the rise. The trout, which had been rising several times each minute for the past quarter of an hour, quit feeding. It was too late to cook a fish anyway; it was late and dark enough that I was ready to call it quits.

The little panic of night coming on with a camp left to make ran across my shoulders and gripped my chest. This claustrophobia of dark defiles had been a lot worse twenty years ago. Tonight, it wasn't as bad, but it wasn't nothing either and it was enough to take the edge off the pleasure of fishing.

Actually, it killed it altogether.

The next morning, I broke camp and pushed off just after daybreak, hoping to avoid being spotted by early boat fishermen. Though no one would think twice about someone in a boat here, a person camping guerilla-style might draw attention. There was something inside me that wanted total anonymity for a few weeks. This had less to do with being on the lam from the FBI—who I doubted would try very hard to look for me, as I wasn't that important—than it did with wanting a leisurely break from my own life for a bit. That's what this trip was really about; a slow float down easy rivers Huck Finn–style. Lots of time for mulling things over; a simple, almost-mechanical exercise keeping the boat in the river, where the water tended to be; total solitude, some fishing, and some stark, clean living far from the temptations of whiskey bars and foie gras.

Besides, if the feds wanted me badly enough, they could have me anyway; they had those kinds of resources and that kind of power. I had done plenty of illegal acts in my life, but couldn't think of anything offhand I regretted or felt sorry about.

At daybreak, a fine mist lingered over the more turbulent sections of the river. In the stillness of morning, the cry of a hermit thrush hung over the woodland. I rowed into the current

The moon illuminates the Missouri River,
Montana. STEVEN GNAM

and pointed the stern downstream. A great blue heron lifted off a back eddy and flew down the river. I could see the sun on the Pioneer Mountains, and to the east, snowfields hidden in the shade of the high country of the Highland Mountains.

Framed by the ten-thousand-foot peaks of the Bitterroot Mountains, the Pioneer range, and the Anaconda-Pintler mountains, the Big Hole River rises in extreme southwestern Montana. It runs north some fifty miles and cuts to the east another thirty or so miles as the heron flies to the Divide Bridge—where I shoved off to begin this journey. Then it turns south—with I-15 more or less paralleling it—to the tiny town of Glen, then away from roads and people, meandering through braided channels to the bigger town of Twin Bridges, where it is joined by the Ruby and Beaverhead and becomes the Jefferson.

Sunlight descended from above the cottonwoods and flooded the river channel. A few midges and caddis fluttered in the oblique light. I moved right along, not stopping to fish. I knew this section of the Big Hole was where I would run into the most people during the approaching Fourth of July weekend and I wanted to get through it as quickly as possible.

Ahead loomed a bridge and, beyond, an outcrop called Maiden Rock. There were a few fishermen and a couple of rubber rafts getting ready to push off. I felt no need for social contact but didn't wish to appear surly either. I pushed hard on the oars, propelling the drift boat as quickly as possible, rowing around their fishing lies, trying not to disturb them. I nodded to the fishermen as I passed.

The river looped to the west and meandered back. Little snakes squirmed and wriggled along the water's edge. These baby snakes were western garters, which are born alive. I would wait out the heat of the day and all the boats it promised on a goosenecked flat. I tied the boat securely to a tree and got out my sleeping pad, a book, my canteen, and a bottle of mosquito repellent.

I napped away most of the day in the shade of juniper trees. The warm summer day cooled in the shadow of midafternoon, and I prepared to push off. The commercial boat traffic had already peaked, and most guides were hurrying their clients to take-out spots where they could back in a boat trailer and head to the saloon.

I maneuvered the *Green Queen* into the current and pulled on the oars, avoiding a line of rocks. The Big Hole River carried more flow here and I moved rapidly downriver. I was passing up some of the most beautiful trout-fishing water I had ever seen, but I was in a hurry to get downstream; I wanted to get past the little towns of Melrose and Glen and away from the highway and boat traffic.

That night I camped in another thicket, and again pushed off at first light. Big cottonwoods lined the riverbank. I stopped once during the morning to fish a tempting riffle that looked too good to pass up. The long tongue of rapids was about three feet deep with an even cobble bottom. I pivoted the boat, passing wide of the trout lies, and tied the *Green Queen* to a big alder root. I crept back upstream to the tail of the riffle. I tied on a fine tippet with two droppers. I tied a small nymph, from my friend Yvon Chouinard, on the end of the leader and two smaller nymphs on the droppers. I gave the nymphs a couple of seconds to sink and took in the slack. The line paused and I struck and was firm to a surging fish. The fight lasted only moments. I had pulled one of the tiny hooks out of the trout's mouth. The next time I was ready. As the fly hesitated, I gently tightened up on the line and was fast to a foot-long rainbow. The trout gave a small leap in the head of the riffle, then sped downstream with the current. I released the bright female trout and climbed back into the *Green Queen*.

I passed families of mergansers at the water's edge. Herons flew ahead of me. An osprey circled. The *Green Queen* passed under the highway bridge. I aimed the boat downstream and

Doug lived off trout and crayfish on
his sixteen-day paddle down to the
headwaters of the Missouri, Montana.
TOM MONTGOMERY

rowed hard, eager to pass the tiny village of Glen. The Big Hole was so shallow this dry July that I banged off a hidden rock. I quickly pivoted the *Green Queen*, facing the drift of the river, and eased the stern of the craft through the rocks. As I cleared the shallow water, I began to push hard at the oars again, propelling myself as fast as I could move the heavily laden wooden dory and still watch out for snags, shallows, and boulders. I kept at the oars for a couple of hours. I drifted past the few buildings in Glen, seeing no one. I was now leaving civilization behind; there wasn't anything downstream until you hit the Beaverhead. I began to breathe easier.

This vague notion of being on the lam, of being on the run from some variety or abstraction of authority or danger, was commonplace in my life; it had been my companion throughout the years of war and peace.

The stench of the fear of death in war was not the same as the gift of life in a grizzly's charge. These events smelled entirely different. I knew this from firsthand experience. In war, you mostly just tried to stay alive. True, your senses and attentiveness were sharpened by scanning the edge of the trees for ambushes. And your fear of dying or being maimed in battle made the daily pleasures of cigarettes and sunsets more precious. But this was not the same as true vitality. Loving life was more than just trying to outlive combat, more than staying alive. It reached for a deeper generosity than the austere gratitude of mere survival.

Below Glen, it was clear running all the way to Twin Bridges. There were no roads along the river and scarcely a human structure unless you counted the diversion dams. I passed another of these human-made barriers, about the fifth major one since putting in at Divide. Here a bulldozed wall of alluvial gravel blocked two-thirds of the river and diverted a third or so of the flow of the Big Hole into a canal leaving the river to irrigate nearby alfalfa fields. These alluvial dams had to be rebuilt after big rains and high water. The damage from the siltation resulting from dozing the river often killed all the fish below for part of a mile and destroyed both the spawning beds and the aquatic life the fish fed on even farther downstream.

The river coursed east. I ducked my head to pass under a low steel bridge for a gravel road, the last for miles. The high banks consisted of cottonwoods alternating with willow flats interspersed with breaks of alder growing along old alluvial channels. Chokecherries crowded the little gullies.

It was a fine, mild day, not hot, just a hint of breeze, a few clouds decorating an immaculate Montana sky. Rowing along the south bank under the trees, I could smell the sun on the hawthorn, chokecherries, and rose hips, the rich redolence of fruit awaiting ripeness. On the larger boulders—the ones at least two feet above the present water level—thousands of empty cases of big stoneflies clung to the rock. The average length of the nymphs, which had hatched about a month ago, was over an inch. These big, meaty bugs, perhaps the favorite trout food in most Montana streams, lay their eggs in the water. The eggs sink into the gravel and hatch into nymphs. Over the course of a year or two, the nymphs undergo several molts into these big suckers, which crawl onto the rocks or onto the branches of streamside bushes. Once they crawl out, they emerge as adults, providing the most exciting fishing on the continent on big dry flies.

Everything was in transition, bugs and plants, the river always moving, changing. I thought about my own appetite for metamorphosis, the image of dying a little death, shedding the old skin, letting it all go. Rowing, like walking, was a meditation. You performed useful work, you paid attention to detail, and—at your best—you got outside yourself to look back in.

By late afternoon, I passed another major dam diverting a big hunk of the river. The flow of the Big Hole was noticeably

Impending trout gluttony: salmon flies
line the streamside vegetation in Montana.
JAKE HAWKES

decreased here, and the *Green Queen* banged over rocks and
scraped over shallows. I had to get out every third of a mile, tie
the bow line around my waist, and lift the bow slightly with the
rope over my shoulder to drag the dory over the shallow heads
of narrow chutes.

I began to wonder if there was going to be enough water in
the river to float me down to the headwaters of the Missouri. The
combination of consecutive drought years and anachronistic water laws that permitted every rancher to withdraw whatever river
water he wanted was having a heavy impact on the Big Hole. It
looked like half the river water was repeatedly diverted every five
or so miles. How long would it be before the entire river dried up?

That evening I made camp in a tiny, lovely clearing in the
middle of a magical little island. Spring runoff would normally
have inundated such an island, but now a grove of cottonwoods
walled in an enchanted glade. It looked like a childhood dream.
But with two years of serious drought and more of low water, a
rich soil had developed, and plant succession had proceeded to
allow for a mossy carpet of lupine and paintbrush.

I had a bottle of Montana Riesling I'd picked up at the bar
in Melrose, the only wine available with a cork in the bottle. I
wanted to use the white wine to poach a Big Hole trout. Plenty of
fish were feeding, but gauging by the splashes, most of them appeared small. I was hungry and needed a sizable fish for dinner.

I walked down the gravelly beach. Several fish were feeding
toward the tail of the island. In the fast, smooth water, I could
see the backs of fish bulging in the current just below the surface.
I flipped the fly upstream and across the channel, gave it a tug
to pull it under the surface, then mended my line. As it reached
the feeding trout, there was a boil and I was fast to a nice rainbow, about a foot long. I guided the trout into the shallow and
beached it on the shore. I whacked it on the head with a stone
and quickly cleaned it. I wanted this one for dinner.

Before packing up my rod, I picked mint from the river's edge, pulled up a few wild onion plants from the marshy end of the island, and grabbed a handful of sage from the higher bank.

Back in my tiny clearing, I kindled a small fire. The last light was fading from the sky. I pulled out four new potatoes from my food bag; my larder was intentionally minimal. I wrapped the potatoes in squares of aluminum foil and placed them at the periphery of the fire; they would roast while the trout poached. I positioned a small skillet balanced between two long rocks and suspended a couple of inches over the fire, which I kept burning with twigs of dead willow. I popped the cork on the white wine and poured a tin cup of Riesling for the cook, then dumped a half inch of wine into the skillet. I placed the wild mint leaves in the wine and then chopped up the corms of wild onion. I mixed the onion with a few leaves of native sage and stuffed the trout with the mixture. When the wine began to steam, I carefully laid the thirteen-inch rainbow trout, cut in half to accommodate the small frying pan, in the wine, fashioning a tent of aluminum foil over the trout. I leaned back on my pad against my sleeping bag and sipped my wine as I studied the window of sky. The brighter stars were coming out. My camp was made, and the tent was up.

My muscles, especially my shoulders and thighs, were sore from rowing, but I felt good. I was content to listen to the soft murmur of water gurgling around the little island. I hooked a new potato out of the fire with a stick and poked a knife into the spud to see if it was done. It was. Condiments were salt for the four tiny potatoes and a squeeze of lemon for the fish. I could smell the hint of mint in the poaching wine and the chives and sage on the trout—a memorable meal.

I awoke to the sound of heron wings. The sun was on the trees; it was later than I was accustomed to getting started. No matter, I had no schedule or any destination other than downstream.

I broke down the tent, packed up the boat, and pushed off about midmorning. Herons lifted off ahead every few hundred yards. I passed six families of common mergansers in the first half hour, including a mother with fifty or so chicks. I don't know much about merganser chick-raising, but this litter had to be the coalescence of several families; I wondered how the birds decided which one should be the adopted mother. Killdeer were also common and dragged their phony wounded wings away from nests at every bend of the river.

Just before midday, the light softened and I became aware of a huge looming cloud edging into the southwestern sky. The cumulus thunderhead dominated the entire southern sky; its slow, steady movement was unyielding. If it continued to drift this way, I'd have to get out of the river. There would be lightning, maybe violent rain or hail; it would be too dangerous to be out on the river.

I entered another little rapid, where the whole river narrowed to a white chute ten feet across. The riverbed was much wider than the narrow channel of actual water. The whiteness of alluvial boulders attested to the rapidly dropping water table. I moved along, enjoying the gusty air, watching the weather move in. I drifted with the current, feeling like I was the river: traveling slowly through the country, smelling the earthy fetor of the Big Hole, feeling the afternoon breeze rise in advance of the big thunderheads, anticipating the wind to stiffen as the storm arrived, blowing hard in the cottonwoods, turning the leaves upside down, white against the distance of darkening sky, imagining the howl of wind and the first splash of rain on the water.

By now, the southern sky was black, and I doubted the storm would miss me. I pushed on the oars. The bow swung outward as it caught the current and I aimed the stern downstream toward Notch Bottom, a name full of possibilities I had always admired.

The wind had picked up and the parched leaves of alder and cottonwood trees were plucked from drought-stricken branches and whipped across the river. Ahead, the river divided into two braided channels. I didn't know which one to take and I didn't want to end up in a dead-end channel where my downstream progress might suddenly be obstructed by a downfall or logjam, especially with a violent storm blowing in. I thought I should probably find a spot to get out of the river and wait out the storm.

In my boat I carried enough rain gear and plastic garbage bags to weather out a little rainstorm, even one of intensity. But this giant thunderhead was big enough to generate considerable wind and lightning, lots of rain, and maybe hail. I needed to find a place to erect the tent where a tree wouldn't blow down on it and where I could sit on an insulating pad in case the lightning got too close.

Off to the right, on the south bank, an out-hanging snag afforded a little harbor and a place to securely tie up the boat. Beyond was an open grove of big cottonwood trees. Bolts of lightning were now raining down in the southern sky and I counted the seconds to see how far away the eye of the storm was: almost fifteen seconds, or three miles. I had about ten minutes to cover the boat and put up a tent. I hurried the tent, pad, and sleeping bag into the trees. I picked a site in the lee of the biggest tree, one that had been hit by lightning and pruned of the hazard of dead branches that might blow off in the wind. I quickly put the dome tent up and tied it to the tree. I stuffed my pad and sleeping bag inside and ran back to the boat to get more gear—enough to wait out the duration of the storm. The first whipped drops of rain stung my face. I was out of time. The storm had arrived.

I dove into the tent just as the deluge abruptly turned into a hailstorm. I zipped up the rain fly and huddled in the center of

A hailstorm approaches the Big Hole River,
Montana—time to get out of the boat.
STEVEN GNAM

the dome tent. Hail pounded the tent, thunderous and growing louder; I wondered if the tent would hold up. I peeked out with the dim instinct of an animal trapped in a collapsing den looking for sanctuary in a nearby cave or under a big log. I could see the full rage of the rare summer ice storm now. The hail ranged in size between big marbles and small golf balls and bounced off the ground like frozen pearls. The cottonwood branches broke the fall of hail only slightly. These ice balls would hurt, and maybe kill you if a big one caught you behind the ear. There was no place to hide. I'd have to stay where I was, hoping the tent held up to the ice barrage. Lightning crashed somewhere close by.

The hailstorm lasted for ten minutes. By then there were two inches of it on the ground. I stepped out into a white landscape. I could hear the painful bellowing of cattle in every direction. Magpies complained loudly; perhaps their nests had been damaged. I wondered why the magpies were so much louder than other birds who were also caught in the storm. A single shaft of sunlight pierced the river bottom. The birds began to sing: red-winged blackbirds, thrushes, and towhees. Ravens croaked. Two hawks circled.

I gathered up an ice chest full of hail. How I wish I had a few beers to cool down. I was proud of the little tent; it had done its job. This tent was a freebie, a gift from an out-of-business outdoor company, one of the first of the dome tents—codesigned by my friend Doug Tompkins. I was impressed. None of my old tents would have stood up to the fierce pounding of big hailstones.

Once more I packed my gear. The hail had melted in the *Green Queen* and I bailed out the water with a plastic gallon milk container with the top cut out around the handle. The river seemed to be growing milkier by the minute. I pushed off and aimed the boat at the right channel, where most of the water flowed. The river divided again and now the channel was only about fifteen feet wide. I dodged overhanging alder branches. A couple hundred feet ahead, an entire cottonwood tree with the leaves still attached blocked the channel. I had come at least a quarter mile down the channel and didn't relish trying to haul the unwieldy boat back upstream. The tree wasn't huge, perhaps ten inches or a foot in diameter. I tied up the boat and got out the three-quarter ax I had carried for just such an occasion. I went to work on the tree.

Twenty minutes later I had chopped the trunk in half twice, opening a six-foot gate through which I lined the dory. I snatched up the oars and continued downstream. The fast, narrow river snaked through trees and bushes. A dark-brown animal surfaced on the water and scampered up on a log. The mink watched me as I drifted up to his log. He disappeared into the brush.

The channel rejoined the others and I steered the Green Queen into what I guessed was deeper water, judging by the currents. The river had risen perhaps a foot and by now it was an opaque milky white. The river divided again and once more I took the channel with the most water in it. Less than an eighth of a mile downstream, I came to a huge cottonwood log spanning the entire channel. This one was three feet across and a foot above the water. There was no way I could get over or through the obstruction.

I stripped off my clothes and re-dressed in only tennis shoes and a T-shirt to protect my shoulders from rope burn. I tied a loop in the bow rope and draped it over one shoulder and under the opposite arm. I stepped into the water, which was colder now from the hail and runoff. I couldn't tell how deep it was except by feeling the bottom with my feet. I tried to haul the boat directly upstream but it was too heavy; I couldn't get enough leverage to pull the Green Queen against the swift current. I tied on another twenty feet of rope and went upstream to the bank, braced against a log, and pulled the dory hand over hand through the deep channel. I repeated this technique when-ever the water was too deep. Two hours later, exhausted and breathing heavily, I had moved the boat back upstream to where the river had divided. Despite the cold water, sweat ran into my eyes. I peeled off my shirt and submerged in the milky river. I air-dried for five minutes and got dressed.

Past Notch Bottom the river continued to rise, though not at an alarming rate, and the color lightened to marl white. I doubt-ed that the color of the river was entirely natural, caused only by the storm. Maybe a diversion dam or two had washed out or someone upstream was bulldozing the river and rebuilding one of the destructive barriers. I could only guess. Great blue herons sat in trees waiting for the river to clear so they could fish again. I passed Biltmore Hot Springs rowing as fast as I could, not for any particular reason, but enlivened by the storm and cutting the tree. And besides, there would be no fishing until the river began to clear, and that could take days.

At the High Road bridge, I hid the boat in a willow thicket and walked a mile east into Twin Bridges. I bought bread, apples, and a pint of VO Canadian whiskey that I sipped on as I walked back to the boat. An osprey sat in a snag above the *Green Queen*. I shoved off back on the river. I poured VO into a tin cup and added a little water, keeping the cup on the floorboards of the drift boat when I had to use the oars. Seven herons perched in a dead tree ahead; they looked like vultures. I toasted the long-legged waterbirds, finishing the cup of whiskey.

The river pulled me steadily away from the pleasant though crowded cloister of buildings comprising the small western town. Ahead, a big river, the Beaverhead, joined the Big Hole from the northeast. Right where the Big Hole River met the Beaverhead, a large beaver slapped the water. There were two wide channels now and I couldn't decide which one to take. At the last moment, I chose the one to the right. I pivoted the boat and stupidly missed a stroke with the oar. The river was swift and muscular now. The current drove the *Green Queen* into a deadhead log that stove in the side and water poured into the boat.

I tried bailing the boat, but the water was coming in too fast. The collision was dumb, but I'd still have to patch the hole. I started looking for a campsite.

Past the confluence with the Ruby and the Beaverhead, the Big Hole ended. The river was now known as the Jefferson. And most of the land along the Jefferson was private and posted. This was a small inconvenience, as no one ever saw my camps. But I still preferred to know where I was, the ownership of the land I stood upon. Most backcountry land in the American West is public land, though very often the people, especially ranchers, who buy the grazing rights to state and federal land treat it as their private domain, using and abusing the land as they see fit and denying access to the public. I consulted my Interagency map; there was a small piece of state land just around the bend. Since I had to sand, glue, and dry the area where I damaged the boat, I wanted to know that I had a right to be there.

It was a lovely camp on a sand clearing separated from the river by low willows. I hammered the shattered plywood hull back into position with a flat rock, then scraped and sanded the boat clean; the break wasn't as bad as I'd thought. I kindled a little fire near the boat to dry the wood so the glue and duct tape would stick. The snow caught up in the vast distance of the Tobacco Root Mountains reflected the last light of day. Snipe winnowed and darted in the evening sky. Most of the milky silt had settled out and the river began to clear to the color of dark whiskey.

Speaking of whiskey—there was some left in the pint of VO. But I wasn't in the mood. In fact, it was time to take a break from the bottle, I told myself. I thought about Ed Abbey. One way to honor a friend who has died from complications of an alcohol-related disease is to quit drinking. I uncapped what was left of the blended whiskey and added its contents to the booze-colored Jefferson.

The next morning, I tested my patch and added an extra layer of heavy-duty duct tape to each side of the hole. It would be two more years before the tape would be replaced with a proper patch. Ahead loomed a trident-shaped voodoo heron tree; six herons perched in the lightning-struck tree and ten more flew by overhead. I had never seen such densities of great blue herons. A flock of young mergansers galloped upstream in a froth of water along the opposite bank.

The Jefferson and Upper Missouri were neither popular floats nor whitewater areas. This was sparsely populated ranch country. I didn't expect to see any other boats or many fishermen on the hundred-mile run of river. Each night I would camp hidden in a grove of cottonwoods or a thicket of willow, like Huck Finn, something I never got to do as a boy. Since I couldn't get off the river, I intended to keep going no matter what; diversion dams, shallows, or rapids. I would rarely be seen—only when passing towns or bridges—and no one would pay any attention to me then. It dawned on me that I could keep going down the river, down the Missouri, past big dams, into the Mississippi, past towns and cities, all the way to the Gulf of Mexico. I could continue to row during the days, forage for food, hunt, fish, and camp hidden by timber or nightfall all the way to New Orleans—an ancient, neglected but tested path for a renegade to stay on the lam in America.

The river was dropping and clearing. Bugs were hatching. At this time in my fishing life, I knew only one trick for beating the hatch when you couldn't match it, and that was to forget about dry flies and fish a big wet fly slightly downstream from the surface activity.

I lifted the rod tip and flung the graceless but effective fly upstream and across, approximating a cast. The stonefly imitation hit the water with a clumsy splash next to the bank just above the rising fish. When the big wet fly reached the lie of the feeding fish farthest downstream, I raised the tip of my fly rod to take the slack out of the line. The line hesitated and I struck. I was fast to a good fish.

The trout made a run downstream taking out line and then bulldogged on the bottom for two minutes at the tail of the pool, then made a fast run upstream. I eased the fish to the edge of the current; a hook-jawed male trout with big brown spots rose to the surface. The brown was about twenty inches long and not very heavy in the body. I had my son Colin's landing net with me, suspended by the elastic around my shoulder. But this fish was too large for the net. No matter, the net was to keep me company, to remind me of the little boy I loved, not necessarily for netting trout. I reached down with the hemostats and twisted the hook. It slid out easily. The trout bolted away.

I moved on down the river in the *Green Queen*. The fishing was hot, and I stopped often to sample it. Just short a mile or so from the Ironrod Bridge, I made a late camp in a small, thick grove of trees.

I had camped short of the bridge because there was a diversion dam just below it. I hadn't seen it, but my map said it was there. I was timing my passage through, over, or around the dam to late morning; I figured I might have to get wet and wanted the sun to be up.

The next morning, I beached the *Green Queen* just above the bridge and walked up to the road to have a look. The river was broad and shallow here; the current had slowed. The diversion dam was just below the high iron bridge. I walked out on the

Doug floats past "the biggest heron rookery
I've ever seen." Jefferson River, Montana.
TOM BAUER

bridge and leaned over a steel beam, checking the dam with my binoculars.

The diversion dam was made of big slabs of concrete bulldozed into position. The cement obstruction had been there for a while. In the middle of the slabs, water surged through the line of debris. This break was about eight or ten feet wide and there was a concrete slab in the middle. The river dropped perhaps six or eight feet in the twenty-foot cascade of water. The problem was that there wasn't a clean run through the gap. Big cement blocks obstructed the channel.

There was no way the boat could pass through the diversion dam without smashing it to pieces on the concrete slabs. The passage between chunks of sharp cement was barely wide enough to accommodate the width of the dory. I would have to unload the *Green Queen*, design some system of pulleys, and line the boat through slowly enough to avoid smashing it against the cement boulders.

I took everything out of the boat and left it on the bank next to the dam. Enough water moved through the gap to provide a cushion against the biggest slab below. If I could ease the boat over the drop-off into the first big boulder, the water would carry it off to the side and down a ten-foot cascade into another slab. As long as the boat wasn't moving too fast, smashing against the rock shouldn't damage it too badly. I abandoned my plans to rig a pulley system and figured I'd use my body, pulling against the line, as a break.

A slick of water rushed through a ten-foot break in the diversion dam, then split into two white tongues of current surging around a half-dozen chunks of cement. The right channel was better, but neither was good.

I could belay the heavy boat until it started down the tongue of water. Then I'd have to let it go and grab the rope and belay again just before it smashed into the second big boulder. I was aiming for a soft smash. The *Green Queen* was also tied to a second longer line to keep it from floating off down the river once it bounced off the second rock.

The boat was poised at the top of the slick. In the river, I held the bow line in a belay around my waist, letting out line an inch at a time. When the stern eased into heavy flow, I let go. The boat roared down the slick into the first boulder. I grabbed the second line and braced myself. The heavy dory pulled me off my feet and hit the rock, sliding off to the right. I lost my footing and went under. When I reemerged, the *Green Queen* was about to smash into the second slab. I seized the line again and hung on as hard as I could. The force of the river against the boat snatched me off my second belay and tossed me into the rocks, ripping my pants and tearing the skin off a shin and forearm. I went under but missed knocking my teeth out on the rocks. When I popped up, I looked downriver and saw my dory floating in the quiet water below.

I reloaded the boat and was on the river again. The Jefferson had noticeably slowed since Divide on the Big Hole in its race to the Missouri headwaters. Here the stream meandered through the middle of a wide valley. Willow flats and cottonwood lined the bank. The river swung east in a broad horseshoe loop. The outer bank was undercut and deep, the bottom graded to gravelly shallows on the inside of the bend. It was a perfect place to fish.

I believed the only fly that would work was the one tied by fishing friend Mike Monroe—which looked like half-butchered chicken. In the middle of the run, I lost this fly, breaking off on a log at the bottom of a five-foot-deep run. I peeled off my clothes and dove repeatedly for the fly. After a few minutes in the water, I grew accustomed to the cold. The river flow pushed me into a slow eddy and I peered under the bank into a fish lie and retrieved my irreplaceable crayfish fly. I looked up from under the snag, the current pressing my body against the log, and watched the lattice of moving light pierced by the dark shaft of a raven flying downstream.

Later, I learned the half-butchered-chicken fly wasn't irreplaceable, and that just about any old, big brown or black thing would work if fished deep, drifting naturally but moving spastically.

I started wading at the top of the U-shaped run. By the time I finished the hundred yards of river, I landed nine fish between thirteen and twenty inches long. The deep, downstream-retrieve technique was irresistible. That afternoon and the next morning I caught seventeen fish between fifteen and twenty-two inches.

I caught so many fish that I quit fishing altogether for a while. Even though I was releasing these fish, I was traumatically hooking and beaching them. I didn't need the fish for food. So why was I still fishing? For sport? As long as I released the trout without killing them, other fishermen could catch them, too. I was subscribing to conventions of the sport and the law. Was the highest use of a trout to be as a prize for sportsmen?

I was, by this time in my life, beyond any notion of "sport" as an appropriate practice in the wild. Yet, I was willing to kill and eat animals. For me, fishing, hunting, and gathering were utilitarian uses of the wilderness. By utilitarian, I mean activity that counts, endeavors that get something real such as food or practical knowledge out of the wild, a purpose for going there more vital than recreation. This was not the same as seeing the wilderness as a giant free supermarket. For me, proper use of the wild implied that the wilderness—or the land, or even the planet—should get something back from our human use, a beneficial symbiosis. This was my somewhat-pompous quandary: If hunting or fishing was supposed to be a contract of reciprocity, what evolutionary or other good is hunting to those animals being hunted?

Here on the Missouri headwaters, seeing myself as "hunter" was an exaggeration of the fact that I was living off the land—gathering mushrooms and catching fish and crayfish for dinner. It had little or nothing to do with sport. My autumnal passion was increasingly sensate and this sensuality was becoming my guide: heron dreaming, the green empathy of becoming the forest, reflecting like the river.

I ran into another diversion dam by Parrot Castle. Once again, I unloaded the *Green Queen* and lined her through the chute. I ruminated on the changing climate: The combination of increasing drought and irrigation had seriously depleted the flow of the Jefferson here. The boat scraped over numerous shallows. I got out many times to drag the boat through channels. Occasionally, there would be a good run and deep pools where the trout congregated. There seemed to be cold groundwater seeping into the river that chilled the temperature of the pools enough to keep the fish alive; I could feel the cool water from the seeps on my toes when I dragged my feet in the water.

Still, the Jefferson and the other rivers of the Missouri headwaters could experience unprecedented fish kills that could decimate the blue-ribbon trout fishery of southeastern Montana. The death of the fish, the maiming of the organic river, was the direct result of human greed, of a modern madness that thought the water was free and unlimited and that believed the rancher's agricultural economic well-being had superiority over all other natural activities.

By this time, I had quit fishing altogether. It didn't seem fair, and I had eaten all the trout and crayfish bouillabaisse I could stomach. Ahead was a point of rocks. An osprey nested on a utility pole in the distance. Across from the outcrop lay a little thicket within a quarter section of state land. I stood up in the boat and snared a branch on the faster-moving, deeper outer bank. I looped the bow line over a big root and pulled myself up the four-foot vertical embankment. My nose eased over the bank for a look.

My heart stopped. A foot from my forehead something moved. I was face-to-face with a huge hissing snake. I figured to take the prairie rattlesnake bite right on the nose. It would leave one ugly scar; my nose might have to be amputated. The big snake's tail vibrated rapidly in the leaves. But the sound was not a rattle because this snake didn't have rattles: it was a bull snake. I started to breathe again. I lay on the bank and looked up through the summer-green hawthorn and cottonwood to the blue sky beyond. The sweet babble of river laughed at me.

The close encounter with the nonvenomous snake brought me a heightened awareness of the beauty all around me. It was good to have dangerous wild neighbors. Living among grizzly bears had made a similar impression on me. Sharing the habitat with animals that sometimes kill or eat humans was the most direct route I knew toward a non-anthropocentric cosmology. How the hell could anyone believe humans were the center of the world when facing venomous reptiles, grizzlies, tigers, lions, jaguars, or polar bears on equal terms and neutral turf?

It would also be useful to retain one's humility during more or less normal daily situations, I thought, conditions only slightly less banal than run-ins with rent-a-cops in shopping malls or a domestic spat. Something to keep in mind the next time I ran into a snake.

During the night, a gentle rain beat against the tent for half an hour. Just before daylight, coyotes cried out across the river. At daybreak, a white-tailed deer splashing noisily across the river awakened me. I looked out the tent door. Fingers of ground fog followed the waterways and a few scudding clouds lay under a high overcast sky. I made coffee, packed up, and pushed off into the current, entering the river's flow.

I drifted past a pair of sandhill cranes, the long-legged birds sauntering and jerking into the alder. Cattails were coming up on the right bank. The current drifted me past an owl, possibly a short-eared, who rose from a stump in the water. He carried a rodent, probably a muskrat, so heavy the big bird struggled to remain airborne.

About midday, a few drops of rain fell. The sky cracked and a shaft of sunlight illuminated the rain in golden light. The river drew me toward a grove of huge cottonwood trees set back from the river on the left bank. The trees towered above the willow scrub field. I could see many stick nests in the upper branches. I held the oars motionless above the water, drifting like a great green leaf bobbing on the skin of the river. The glade opened as I drifted past and I looked at a hundred stick nests in four big trees, a third or more of them occupied.

The current pushed me out and down, slowly turning the stern toward the rookery, the biggest I had ever seen by a factor of four. I drifted past, eye to eye with dozens of herons, two or three to a nest mostly, young birds standing on stick nests, a scene I might have expected in the Serengeti.

The *Green Queen* and I floated in and out of days. The river buoyed us up and down, the current catching us in an eddy then releasing, letting go. I rowed on, the flake of boat and man floating like the sheet ice of spring melt. Though my hands were calloused with furrows of thick skin, my body felt hypersensitive to the world around it. I remembered the time a bark scorpion, a little desert arachnid packing a nasty wallop, stung me on the little finger and how the nerves were hypersensitized for weeks; even running lukewarm tap water over the finger felt unbearable, like fire.

Now it was less painful, less tactile, yet otherwise much the same. I could feel through my skin the minuscule changes of temperature manifested by passing changes in vegetation reflecting the heat. I heard the faint siliceous rustle of fine sediment suspended in the current grazing the green side of the boat. With my eyes closed, I could sense the changing currents and navigate

Sandhill cranes grace a Missouri
headwater meadows. Montana.
DANITA DELIMONT/ALAMY

sightless into the main channels. I had quit killing fish and cray-fish. I became a total vegetarian. The lack of booze gave me an uncommonly clear head. Modern living had numbed and blind-ed me to the audible and olfactory universe of birds and insects whose messages were now arriving on every breath of breeze.

About midday I beached on a gravel bar separating a wil-low-lined side channel from the main branch of the Jefferson. It was hot. I stripped off my clothes and swam for a few minutes, then stood in the sun to dry. A nest of tent caterpillars in the willows hung over the water. I watched one of the larval worms drop off and float downstream.

Below the great colonial heron rookery, the river took me under another bridge, past alfalfa fields irrigated by noisy pumps sucking up the dwindling water flow through big rubber hoses, past ugly levees and open wounds on the land made by bulldozers and backhoes.

Warmer-water fish now occupied the slower holes and the tailouts of longer runs. Schools of suckers and an occasional big squawfish darted away from the shadow of the *Green Queen* passing over. The river pushed past the towns of Whitehall and Cardwell and drove easterly, slicing a canyon through a little range of limestone mountains. The grassy slopes rolled up into the wedges of timber lodged in draws and on north slopes.

The caves of Lewis & Clark Caverns State Park lay on the north shore just ahead. I had taken my family—Lisa, Laurel, and Colin—there the summer before; it had been my first trip into a big cave since I had gone down alone into a tunnel complex in Vietnam and had stumbled into a cache of recently buried bodies. Though I hadn't yet put that experience behind me, I had been able to enjoy the caverns with my children who, at six and eight, had become both my peers and teachers.

My children encouraged my childishness and brought out the best in it. My greatest joys tended to be childish. I had really never acted my age and now my counterparts were my own kids; I gave in to them with all the courage I could muster.

This Huck Finn trip on the river was somehow intended to return to that world. My cloistered camps in tiny willow thickets along the Big Hole and Jefferson were exactly the same nest-like refuges my kids would have sought out for play: little, snug, concealed homes where you can see things coming. At night, I would lie safe in my tent—my little nylon fort—hidden among the thickets of young cottonwood, listening for approaching animals, remembering that sweet boyish comfort. I wanted both the openness of the child and the confidence of an adult. My guides here were my children and old Ed, whom I so admired for his bravery, both physical and spiritual.

Walking the wide-open terrain of anarchy in full view of ideological and academic snipers blasting away from the high ground took guts. There were intellectual risks in the merging of disparate ideas. The iconoclast Abbey took chances; he laughed at odd times, irreverently seeking new ideas or images he thought essential to survival of the planet.

Downstream of the caverns, the river bent away from the road and sliced a gentle gorge through the hills south before dumping out onto the valley of the confluence of the Jefferson, the Madison, and the Gallatin Rivers—the Missouri headwaters.

An old homestead stood on a bench above the river next to an abandoned railroad. I put in early in the day, wanting to linger here upriver in the last roadless section of the Jefferson. I got out a bar of soap and took a bath.

Later, I pitched my tent in the deserted orchard. A great horned owl hooted me to sleep. The audible song of the river beckoned me downstream. In my sleep, I resisted. The anchor of dreams held me firm to the cobble terrace, drawing me deeper into the alluvial earth. The owl returned.

Then it was daylight.

The pull of the river, the relentless tug of gravity—I eddied up below a narrow tongue of rapids along a slow hole where I beached the boat for the night. The last night out.

Sixteen days after launching from Divide, I landed just below a bridge near Three Forks, fifteen pounds lighter—the result of no booze, a trout and crayfish diet, and lots of rowing. I hid the *Green Queen* in the willows, hitched into Three Forks, and found a phone. I called my wife: no news about the FBI was good news. I was looking forward to being married again. Then I called my friend David Quammen who lived upstream on the fork called the Gallatin. Please come pick me up, I implored. I'm at the headwaters.

STALKING POLAR BEARS WITH DOUG TOMPKINS

During the summer of 1991, Doug Tompkins picked me up on a landing strip near Vancouver, British Columbia, and we flew north in his Cessna 206, eventually crossing Canada, southwest to northeast.

Doug and I had never met before; our mutual friend Yvon Chouinard arranged this meeting. In a week or so, Doug and I would join up with another member of our group, Rick Ridgeway, in Edmonton and we'd all head up to polar bear country.

Compared with my well-traveled friends, I was a novice at flying. I had spent considerable time on the ground bushwhacking around the countryside, but I'd never had the luxury of flying in a small plane. Doug piloted us over the vast expanses of the

Previous spread: A Twin Otter plane lands with another load after dropping off the crew on Somerset Island in the Canadian High Arctic. RICK RIDGEWAY

Canadian wilderness, getting the big view of the uninhabited lands of British Columbia—a place we were all trying to preserve. Doug was also a world-class kayaker and wanted to visit the Queen Charlotte Islands, as they were called at the time, and rent kayaks. I neglected to inform him I had scarcely seen the inside of a kayak.

The general plan was to meander north, flying up the coastal ranges of British Columbia, toward the Queen Charlotte Islands, checking out wild valleys and rivers on the way. This was, of course, on the opposite corner of the continent from the High Arctic, but this didn't bother Doug; the meandering was both business and fun. He was always on the lookout for big uncut landscapes, and if he liked them, he'd buy them or find someone to protect them. And Doug kept an eye out for white frothing water, rivers so deadly fast he could add them to his list of "first descents." This was his life.

But our jaunt was a side trip. The rough plan was to spend no more than four or five days in the Queen Charlottes, then hop back into Doug's single-engine airplane and head east, taking a couple of days to check out strategic uncut forests in the interior of British Columbia and Alberta, and then drop into Edmonton, where we would load our gear on a commercial jet and fly to the town of Resolute on Cornwallis Island. There we would pick up some Inuit intelligence on where the belugas were, and head into white bear country.

That was my deal: I had agreed to accompany a beluga whale expedition to the High Arctic—the Canadian island country west of Greenland. That land was polar bear country and a few members of the group were understandably nervous. My job was to be the polar bear guy, to walk point in white bear country. I had invited my pals Doug, Rick, and Bart Lewis to join us.

I was taking the bear job seriously. The pay wasn't much— the price of a plane ticket—but I figured I owed both my friends and the bears a bloodless trip with no casualties on either side. The problem was I didn't know much about polar bears. In fact, outside of the ethnographic and scientific literature, I knew next to nothing. I had seen a few polar bears far out on the pack ice twenty years ago, but nothing since.

———

Doug lands on a deserted runway at Sandspit in the Queen Charlottes and we shoulder our backpacks and hitchhike into town. We rent kayaks and slide into the Skidegate Channel, which cuts through the island archipelago from east to west. A broad band of blue mussels, limpets, and horse barnacles run along the shoreline, indicating the tide to be near its lowest point. We time our paddle in the narrow channel to the rising tide, hoping to reach the midpoint in time to ride the ebb tide down the other side.

Beyond the slate landscape of sea and rock looms the muted green forest of the Pacific Northwest—fir, cedar, and Sitka spruce that reach up into the low clouds from an understory of alder and fern.

Paddling my rented sea kayak frenetically, I gain a slow yard or two on Doug Tompkins, who glides smoothly up the Skidegate. We make camp in a back bay and I follow the little creek up beyond the brackish water to fill my canteens with fresh water. Near the bank are several bear poops from last fall, berry scats from a very big bear. The local Haida told us that there are no brown bear or grizzlies on the islands, but that the black bear grow huge. Black bear are relatively harmless, but I am already thinking about my approach to an encounter with the white bear.

Doug and I run with the tide down the western half of the channel. It begins to drizzle, and then rain hard. We pull into a cove and struggle to light a fire. I use all my experience; I carefully prepare fire sticks and get a well-tended blaze going in the downpour. I am trying to show my new friend that I am worth something after he's discovered that I don't know shit about kayaking.

After pitching the tent, we walk down the beach and find a bear track, another big black bear. I mutter that at least here in the Queen Charlottes we don't have to worry about grizzlies. I confide in Doug that I am a bit edgy about meeting our polar bears, reportedly the most predacious of all bear species, and that I don't know much about them.

Brown bears are a different story: I have spent a good chunk of my life living with grizzly bears and want to believe this experience will allow me to be a "quick study" when dealing with the white bears. After all, polar bear evolution probably followed the needs of a Siberian brown bear that wandered north on the ice 350,000 years ago and started hunting seals. This evolution and de-evolution may have happened twice, and is happening still today. Brown and polar bears can interbreed and their offspring can reproduce. In the age of global warming, the white bear may fold his genes back into the brown bear. Both species share an adaptive intelligence; they are flexible and have a knack for pioneering new habitats and adapting to new situations.

Ursus arctos and *Ursus maritimus* both exhibit a cognitive complexity. Grizzly and polar bears are aware of their own track-making. Grizzlies traveling to den sites during a heavy snow walk backward carefully in their own tracks, suddenly leap off a trail onto a rock or behind a bush, or avoid leaving their paw prints in muddy areas. One of the more disconcerting experiences in nature is to have a bear set up an ambush for you. This has happened to me twice with grizzlies, though I avoided the traps. It's rare but not unknown.

East of our location in British Columbia, during the winter of 1970, a Doig River First Nation hunter found the tracks of a very large grizzly; he wanted to kill the bear for the animal's prime winter coat. He followed the tracks to a head-high mossy hummock, behind which the bear had circled and waited to ambush the man. The male grizzly killed and partially devoured him. That's about all we know about this attack, but you wonder about a malicious intelligence lurking inside that prime winter coat.

Polar bears are generally considered by First Nations people to be more tractable than brown bears—less nervous and even a docile animal by comparison. The difference is that, while grizzlies are truly omnivorous and have diets that lean toward the vegetarian side of the table, the carnivorous white bear is an effective predator. Polar bear attacks on humans reflect this: About two-thirds of the deaths and injuries inflicted by white bears on man have been predatory. Uninterrupted polar bear attacks tend to result in the human victim being eaten.

I tell Doug that I seem to work out my fear of bears in my dreams, where grizzlies threaten me in cabins or the outposts of civilization, but my little nightmares have an uncanny resemblance to real polar bear predations on humans. White bear attacks on people often take place on the edges of industrial culture: out on the drill rigs, the geological camps, the scientific stations, or on displaced pods of ecotourists or biologists—a reality lingering beneath the fear.

In the town of Churchill, Manitoba, a mistake of geography caused the voracious truck of commerce to plop a grain-exporting seaport on the site of an ancient migratory route of polar bears. By fall, the bears, who are hungry, invade the town and feed at the dump. In 1983, a Churchill man closed a bar and walked down a street with his pockets full of scavenged meat from a burned-down hotel. A white bear caught him in the dark from behind, grabbed him by the head, and shook him to death like a dog with a rat.

Polar bears feed at a rubbish dump in
Churchill, Manitoba, Canada. L. LEE RUE/
MINDEN PICTURES

Other attacks took place farther from civilization. During a midmorning in January 1975, on a drilling platform in Canada's Beaufort Sea, a worker was bending over cutting ice off a doorway when a five-year-old male polar bear hit him without warning, a blow so sudden and silent that workers twenty feet away, inside, heard nothing. By the time the man was missed, the bear had dragged him a mile away and had stopped to eat him.

This was the typical pattern of polar bear attacks. Earlier, in 1973, another white bear snatched a worker from a tractor near Kendall Island in the same sea. The pattern of this and other attacks were similar: a silent blow to the head in the dark of winter, delivered from ambush with no warning, just outside the door of the camp, rig, or outhouse. These attacks are predatory; the bear is often a hungry young male.

I know that polar bears are cautious of Eskimos, and also of walrus on land, though the white bear will sometimes stalk either species. Of all animals that sometimes kill and eat humans, no species has as many strategies for success as the bear, especially the white bear. Not that they are designed to accomplish this purpose; on the contrary, all these animals know that stalking the upright ape involves considerable danger. But sometimes it happens. In the case of the polar bear, the strategies for human predation have mostly evolved around its chief prey animal, the ringed seal, a marine mammal with huge eyes and keen hearing.

The white bear kills people the same way it kills the seal, with bites or blows to the head or neck. Sometimes, it appears that polar bears mistake humans for seals. An Austrian tourist was attacked in 1977 when he poked his head out the door of his tent to check on a noise he had heard. The white bear pulled the man out and ate him while his tented companions looked on helplessly.

The kind of fear this produces is palpable: the vestigial fear of being hunted, perhaps left over from our African roots, from our time on the savanna. I wonder about the Eskimo hunter out on the ice, crouched over the breathing hole waiting for a seal, clinging to his spear in the dim or absent light of winter, listening for the hairy padded footsteps of the silent white bear.

We paddle out the west end of the channel. Doug checked out the clear-cuts: This is not what he is looking for. Doug tells me of his love of wild forests, of his faith in deep ecology. In a back bay, we make one last camp. I go fishing, using a stiff broken rod I found in a garbage can in Vancouver. I jig up a couple of greenlings for dinner, then tie on a lure and cast among the kelp where king salmon are jumping. A huge Chinook salmon grabs the lure and explodes from the kelp bed and heads out to sea. It's the biggest salmon I've ever hooked. I hold on to the lousy rod; the fish pulls me and tows my kayak out into the heavy current of the main channel. Local fishing and crab boats roar through here and buzz any kayak at full speed just for the fun of it. I point the rod at the fish and break off just in time, as a crab boat zooms by to swamp me. I make a stroke at the last moment and point the bow toward the big waves. Assholes.

———

It's time to get out of here and fly to Alberta. From Edmonton, we'll board a commercial plane north to Yellowknife and then the High Arctic.

We fly east and south, meandering in and out of huge pristine valleys. Doug is enjoying himself, finding rivers to run and forests to protect. I look for landmarks; I think I can make out the Dean River. Below, snow cornices delineate the watershed of a lovely glacial valley, long white serpents of wind-driven snow hug the ridges. Everything but the permanent snowfields and these remnant cornices has melted in the warm sunlight of late July.

It's a beautiful clear day for flying. The plane climbs south, over a low divide. A small herd of mountain sheep escapes the hordes of insects by bedding on the snow on a broad patch of cornice. I lean out the window and see fresh bear tracks traveling along the snow cornice. The grizzly tracks veer sharply off to the left down into the head of another valley. It looks like the bear was traveling to another seasonal range. Grizzly bears use well-traveled trails and traditional routes when moving from one section of their range to another, but they sometimes take shortcuts, too. I once tracked a grizzly that took advantage of a recent forest fire to take a shortcut to the next drainage. Polar bears may do this also, out on the ice where there is open ice and soft spots. How do they know where they're heading if they've never been that way before? Taking a shortcut, for grizzlies or polar bears, is to go beyond memory. The animal must have some kind of map of the country tucked away in its consciousness.

Polar bears may travel astonishing distances; a bear tagged near Spitsbergen Island showed up two thousand miles to the southwest a year later. Movements of a hundred miles a day have been recorded. But on the ice, with no apparent landmarks in an ever-changing topography of ice and floes, how do they find their way? This travel would be difficult enough in the mountains and forests, but to do so amid the shifting floes and drifting ice goes beyond any consciousness I can imagine.

We make small talk in the cockpit, about music, books, and women. And the mundane: my love of dangerous wild animals and the new navigation system Doug has installed on his plane but hasn't used yet. My eight-foot hickory shaft is in the back of the plane and I tell Doug about my decision to carry a spear into polar bear country rather than the usual rifle or shotgun. A friend forged the nine-inch iron spearhead, knowing what I needed it for and how I intended to use it—as a pike, mounted on a stout wooden shaft of suitable length (I measured a live, captive fourteen-hundred-pound Kodiak bear to obtain this critical measurement). I am intentionally breaking the law by refusing to carry a rifle and packing a spear—that Yvon Chouinard skeptically tested over his knee and couldn't bend—with my specially forged spearhead instead. The only time this defensive weapon would be used is at the conclusion of a polar bear charge. The theory is that you anchor the stern of the shaft on the ground and aim the tip of the spear toward the narrow chest of the white bear, who theoretically impales himself on it by the force of his charge—though of course the odds are not in your favor.

My decision to carry a spear was made earlier in the spring, after considerable research and much reflection. The usual advice, which is law in most quarters, is to carry a big-bore firearm for bear. I disagree. I was recruited for this trip because of my expertise with wild bears and I had experienced dozens of close calls with grizzlies, too many to buy into this fatuity about guns. None of these bears had touched me. Furthermore, I consider it unethical for us to voluntarily invade the last homeland of wild polar bears and then kill them if events do not unfold to our advantage. At the same time, I hate being defenseless.

This argument about guns and bears lies perilously close to the cherished and near-religious beliefs concerning the roots of dominion and masculinity in America. When is it OK to take another life in defense of your own life, your family, or your property? When do you know that others are true threats? Does this include killing a thief stealing your hubcaps? Or just in defense of life? Or when we feel we're being threatened?

Today, humans in the so-called civilized world tend to fear all that is unknown, which increasingly encompasses much of the natural world, including animals like bears. There are two basic camps: Either you believe that human life has more intrinsic value than the bear's life or you do not. If you think it's OK to kill any bear you think might possibly be a threat or a danger, the discussion is over.

The mundane side of the gun argument is that a firearm will get you into more trouble than it will get you out of. And short of shooting the bear that is actively chewing on you, it is never quite clear when to begin shooting. Most of the official bear literature speaks of the necessity of guns for shooting charging grizzlies. Grizzly bears that charge are mostly mothers with cubs that will stop short of you if you inoffensively stand your ground. So, when do you begin shooting?

My judgment to carry a spear resolves all these questions. I consider myself responsible for all my companions should an encounter with a white bear grow critical. That was what I agreed to do: walk point. The bedrock assumption, never discussed, that keeps my carrying the spear from becoming something other than a campy joke, is that you need to be willing to die.

—

We fly out of the Rocky Mountains into the high plains of Alberta. Below is First Nation Country—Blood, Tsuut'ina, and Piikani. Unlike the insular Europeans in their concrete teepees, the Nations of the high plains deliberately courted confrontations with grizzly bears during times of passage: vision quests and wisdom seeking. You sought the bear to get something from it, because if you lived, you came away with wisdom. In such encounters, you offered up your whole life; all your talents and instincts focused on the moment. If you survived—and each time it was an open question—you walked away complete in soul and utterly alive. The confrontation was so intimately personal you sometimes never spoke of it again. To survive such an engagement was always a gift from the bear. The Eskimos of old also deliberately sought out the white bear because the polar bear was "the one that gives power."

The sun is setting behind us and the Cessna drops toward the landing strip in Edmonton. Actually, it is getting dark. I can see the lights of the city ahead. Doug has the manual out for his

Doug walks point in polar bear country,
Canadian High Arctic. DOUG TOMPKINS

new automated navigation system. We are getting really close. I look over Doug's shoulder at the manual. The big print reads: "Getting Started."

———

We find our friends Rick Ridgeway and Bart Lewis. At the Edmonton airport we are joined by Jim Nollman, whose interest is beluga whales. We fly north to Yellowknife, then to Resolute where we sort through our gear. This island country is known as the High Arctic; the town of Resolute sits on the edge of Cornwallis Island. To the south, across a vast strait of pack ice, lies uninhabited Somerset Island, where we hear there is an ice-free fjord full of beluga whales.

The weather closes in. We have to kill a day or two before a bush plane can fly us across the ice and land us on Somerset. Inuit biologists take us in and show us the ruins of thousand-year-old Thule sod houses built around bowhead whale bones. They were constructed about the same time as the Anasazi cliff dwellings of the Southwest. Later, the Inuit take us to their lab, a Quonset hut by the sea. They had been diving below the ice and had brought up a pile of clams, for food as well as research. They shared the catch. Walrus graze on siphons at depths of twenty to forty feet in places. The walrus dive below the ice and chew off the siphons of shellfish sticking up from the bottom, sucking up vast quantities of clams in a single dive. Later, the Inuit biologists share walrus-clam soup with us: They had opened the siphon-stuffed stomach of a freshly killed walrus, poured the mildly acidic contents into a pot, heated it up, and served it with crackers and black pepper.

———

Finally, we land next to the fjord on Somerset Island. The scientist assembles his tent and camping gear while the rest of us unload the Beaver bush plane. The plane departs and I put to-gether my polar bear spear: soaking the sinew in water, inserting the iron spearhead into the slot, and then lashing it tight with wet rawhide that should dry and shrink. The last touch is to screw a sharp metal point into the end opposite the spearpoint where it can anchor on the frozen ground or ice.

The government disagreed with my plan, of course, and they assigned an Inuit hunter to accompany us with his gun. Once the Inuit hunter checks out my spear, he decides I am serious, and we become friends. As the midnight sun heads into the west, he shares a belt of Canadian whiskey from his flask with me.

I hadn't tried out a spear on a bear yet, but the Inuit had once. When he was thirteen, a polar bear wandered into his vil-lage from the ice. The boy and his cousins unchained the dogs, then rushed out with their spears to meet the bear. While the dogs circled and nipped at the big bear, the boys thrust with their spears. My Inuit pal finally threw his spear and was given credit for the kill.

The Inuit hunt polar bear for fur and food, one of the few remaining traditional peoples who intentionally and regularly seek out big predators. You wouldn't want to try this without some really good dogs.

Doug Tompkins had an interesting conversation with the Inu-it hunter about the Native's right to hunt any animal at any time: Doug asked if all the polar bears were reduced to near extinction, would he still shoot the last one? The Inuit was adamant in his right to kill off the last bear, even into extinction. They went back and forth for some time and I could see Doug was shaken.

Both Tompkins and I, in our different approaches, rely upon Indigenous people for our conservation work, for their advice and wisdom. But here Doug had isolated a bedrock contradic-tion, when cultural traditions, especially ancient ones, bump into a firm wall such as species extinction.

We end up with a lot of time on our hands in this magic land-scape of ice, whales, caribou, and musk ox: The sun circles the landscape and our expedition leader, after concluding his beluga whale research objective in the first couple of hours, settles into his tent to read a thick book titled *Reality*.

I learn to spot polar bears out on the ice pack; their coat has a slight yellowish hue, a different color from the ice. One day, I spot seven at once. I impress my Inuit friend by predicting when other bears are present, based on the behavior of a mother polar bear and her two cubs. I know this from my grizzly bear work.

A quarter mile to the south of my tent three white flecks are moving directly toward me across a contrasting canvas of brown and green tundra. They are bears. Through my binoculars I can see a mother polar bear and her two cubs. They will pass inland of my tent, a hundred feet away near the foot of the bluff. I pick up my spear and head to a better vantage point, a moss-covered hummock of ancient bowhead whale bones, the remains of a thousand-year-old Thule-culture sod house.

The white bear family ambles into a little ravine a hundred yards away, still heading my way. They move fluidly with un-imaginable grace and beauty. Holding the eight-foot-long spear in my right hand, I grab a handful of lichen and moss with my left.

Like Antaeus, the giant of Greek mythology, invincible while touching the Earth, I have to be on the ground, holding tight to the world, always sharing the land with wild animals that hold down the same living skin of the Earth with the fierce weight of their paws.

Only whale bones remain of a thousand-
year-old Thule sod house near Resolute
Bay, Canada. The Thule people migrated
from Siberian tiger country in the Russian
Far East to the North American Arctic
around the birth of Christ. UNIVERSAL
IMAGES GROUP NORTH AMERICA
LLC/ALAMY

Previous spread: A black mother spirit bear catches a fresh salmon for her white cub in the Great Bear Rainforest, British Columbia. IAN MCALLISTER

Above: Doug, Karen McAllister, and Dennis Sizemore (left to right) fish for dinner near Princess Royal Island in midcoastal British Columbia. IAN MCALLISTER

SPIRIT BEARS

During the 1990s and early 2000s, I made numerous trips to British Columbia, mostly to support Round River Conservation Studies students by giving campfire pep talks and writing magazine articles supporting the conservation efforts. I had cofounded the nonprofit group and served as board chair for twenty-five years. A few trips were solo, traveling by canoe or kayak and living off the land; others were shared with friends on their sailboat or with Captain Joseph Bettis aboard the *Sundown*. The following story occurred during that time.

———

The current in the Aaltanhash River plunges over a small bedrock sill and deposits its sediment load in a small delta. In the mud at the foot of the waterfall are fresh tracks of black bear and gray wolf, though gray wolves in these parts are sometimes black and black bear are occasionally white.

We slip into our canoe and push off. Chum and pink salmon explode in the shallow tail of the run. I steer the small craft down a black tongue of water into the next pool, where the river, on the east side of the Princess Royal Channel in British Columbia, levels out into a mile-long stretch of quiet water before the next set of cascades dumps into the tidal flat of the fjord.

My wife, Andrea, is in the bow and Karen McAllister squats midcraft between two struts. We duck under an ancient deadfall of red cedar cushioned with a jade cover of moss, paddling quietly, drifting when possible, down the fathom-deep tannic river. Ravens croak and a belted kingfisher squawks a loud complaint. Ahead, an immature bald eagle rises off a towering snag of Sitka spruce. A single tail feather separates from the bird and falls away, swaying as it descends. The scattered golden light in the Canadian sunshine filters through the muted green of western hemlock, cedar, and spruce. I J-stroke into an eddy and scoop up the mottled feather—a good omen.

A half mile downstream, we round a bend and freeze: on the right bank, a plump black bear browses on huckleberries. We drift motionlessly toward the bear, which hasn't seen us. The bear checks out a chum salmon carcass but leaves it where it lies; the fishing is better downriver. He is walking atop a log, grazing on the streamside vegetation, as we drift alongside him. His head reappears with a mouthful of grass and forbs, and we hold our breath: The bear, though fewer than twenty feet away, hasn't spotted us yet. This is natural. Danger doesn't drift down the Aaltanhash in a red plastic log in this bear's universe. We float away from the bear and, suddenly, he sees us. His ears pop up, his mouth falls open, and a mouthful of grass falls into the water. We suppress our giggles. After about thirty seconds of sizing us up, the bear decides to ignore us, and goes back to browsing. He behaves as if he has never seen a human, as if he has yet to learn to fear humans—a situation that may soon change.

This bear, though his coat is black, is a "spirit bear," a race of coastal mainland black bears named for the one in every ten that is born white. The white bears are not albinos; their eyes are dark. Rather, all the spirit bears (also known as Kermode bears) carry a recessive gene that causes these white-colored individuals. A white-phase mother may have three black cubs, or a black-phase mom could have cubs born white, black, and cinnamon. The range of the spirit bear, which some experts consider a subspecies of *Ursus americanus*, extends north to Kaien Island and south to Vancouver Island. Today, most all are found on Princess Royal, Gribbell, and Pooley Islands or the adjacent mainland coast. They depend on salmon, which thrive only in cool, clean stream water, and their presence here speaks more clearly than anything else of the health of these pristine coastal river valleys.

These valleys also grow the big trees coveted by timber companies. And now, with the more commercially viable, easily accessible old-growth forests to the south logged and cheap timber harder to come by, the timber industry is looking north to the realm of the spirit bear.

The watersheds of the central coast of British Columbia contain the last great temperate rainforests left on the continent. The ecosystem is born of maritime winds that blow inland against the coastal mountain ranges, trapping moisture in the valleys. To date, most news of conflict in these rainforests has come out of southern British Columbia—like Clayoquot Sound on Vancouver Island, where, after decades of fighting, First Nations and conservation groups have slowed and contained a forestry industry onslaught against giant Sitka spruce, towering red cedar, and ancient western hemlock. But to the north, at the center of what is known as the Great Bear Rainforest, battle lines have formed over still-untouched watersheds of considerable size and ecological importance. Most are unknown to outsiders. Much of the biological diversity of the region lies in these valleys. These undisturbed lowland forests, dozens of them, hold a mosaic of avalanche scars and thickly forested slopes; they hold the plants and salmon eaten by black and grizzly bears; and they hold ancient trees—the trees sought after by timber interests.

Conservation efforts to save the temperate rainforests in commercial timber country is frustrating; you win a small victory in one drainage and the forest industry clear-cuts another forest next door. You can win many times only to lose once and the entire ecosystem is gone. Edward Abbey cautioned me on this, reminding us to be "a part-time crusader, a halfhearted fanatic," saving the other half for enjoying what we are fighting for: the wilderness.

We are traveling with Karen and Ian McAllister, who live near coastal Bella Bella on the midcoast of British Columbia. They sail on their comfortable sailboat. Though I have been traveling these wild provinces for decades, I have never visited Princess Royal—the principal spirit bear island. The island is just down this ocean inlet, we passed it on the way in to the Aaltanhash. I'd like to see a white bear, visit the Khutze River estuary, go to Pooley Island where wolves fish for salmon, and sneak into spirit bear habitat. I know that these extremely elusive creatures are rarely sighted.

Just before dusk, we hear wolves howl. I paddle the small canoe toward the inlet and jig for fish. I catch two decent quillbacks and a greenling. I quickly fillet the fish and use the carcasses to bait a crab pot.

On the morning of our departure, I dart out to the crab pot and pull it up: it is crawling with Dungeness crabs. I keep three big males. I throw together the boiled and picked crabmeat with some egg, mayonnaise, hot sauce, and seasoning, then dust the crab cakes in pancake flour and fry them in butter until golden. Breakfast is over and we set sail, heading out toward the Princess Royal Channel. A dark, swift bird sweeps out of the sky and strikes a glaucous gull. White feathers erupt from the gull, but it manages to land on the water. Ian says the dark raptor is

Wolves fish for salmon in the Great
Bear Rainforest, British Columbia.
IAN MCALLISTER

a Peale's peregrine, one of the small falcons that nests on the outer coast.

We motor and sail out and up the coast into the shipping lanes. This is the Inland Passage favored by cruise ships and barges, and we pass a huge self-dumping log barge carrying an entire valley's worth of dead trees. Heavy swells roll in from the outer ocean, so we dart inland, taking a narrower but smoother channel. Beyond the thin fringe of timber left along the shoreline, window dressing for international cruise-ship passengers, lie massive clear-cuts.

On the way back south we turn into the Khutze River fjord. Toward the end of the inlet, the estuary and tidal flats swarm with bald eagles and gulls. Waterfalls cascade from every direction into this cathedral of a valley. Clouds of white kittiwakes emerge from a scudding haze upriver; rising behind is a line of larger, darker bald eagles of every age. The flocks of gulls and kittiwakes divide like flecks of white dust blowing around stands of towering Sitka spruce. It is a scene of great power.

At 560,000 acres, Princess Royal is the fourth-largest island in the province. Its topography is subdued compared with the steep-sided fjords across the channel on the mainland. Low scrub forests, bogs, and lakes cover much of the island; most of the commercial timber—there isn't that much of it—lies in sheltered old-growth valleys, where white bears and black wolves dine on numerous salmon runs.

We head south; we will return to Princess Royal Island in a few days. At the southeast tip of Pooley Island, a fresh, A-frame-shaped clear-cut angles up the steep slope; we'll see more of them before the day is out. Halfway down the channel, we swing into James Bay to anchor for the night. A grove of huge Sitka spruce grows in the shelter of the towering granite cliffs above us. A chalk-white beach, which we visit to gather clams for chowder, signals an ancient midden site. The intertidal rectangular lines of rock mark prehistoric fish traps—constructed centuries ago by the ancestors of today's First Nations—that still wash in the gentle surf.

The Indigenous population of the coast has occupied the mainland for at least 10,000 years at places like Namu. But on the outer archipelago southwest of Bella Bella, Heiltsuk archaeologists have found evidence of human fire pits that are 14,000 years old. This means these people came by sea, boating down the glaciated coast from Beringia, after the ice started to melt about 14,700 years ago. The younger occupation, such as that at Namu, may have come from the mainland, down the ice-free corridor from Alaska to Montana. Whether these two separate migrations ever shook hands is one of our great archaeological mysteries.

Later, we head north through birds, past mew gulls, rhinoceros auklets, kittiwakes, and an occasional marbled murrelet. The thin mist of a humpback whale blow evaporates in the morning fog. To the north, subalpine ledges sprout a thin green layer of sedges. A half-dozen white mountain goats decorate the wild landscape.

A small river tumbles into the surf at the edge of Princess Royal Island. We go in, though we are not certain if we are trespassing on private land or not. The tidal flat is littered with bear food. The fetor of rotting dog salmon floats heavily on the breeze. Raven and eagle feathers lie on the tide line. The bulbous head of a harbor seal appears momentarily on the skin of foam where the mottled white backs of spawned-out salmon twist listlessly in the current. We follow deep footprints of generations of grizzly bear walking in the same tracks into the meadow at the edge of the estuary. The headless carcasses of salmon line the banks and black bear tracks are everywhere. The meadow is full of grizzly bear digs; the most recent appear to be for the corms and roots of angelica and lovage, fall food in this country.

A brown bear dines on berries on
Princess Royal Island, British Columbia.
IAN MCALLISTER

The stream is stained chestnut from the rich organic matter. A few salmon are in the river, but the bears here are feeding on forbs and berries. We stop at a bear-marked tree. Fine guard hairs, caught up in the bark and resin, indicate black bears of several colors reside in this valley. We extract a slender bundle of three-inch-long hairs. They are pure white.

We spend the rest of the day looking for the white bear, finding only hair and a quart of yellow chanterelle mushrooms. I see wolf sign and an older grizzly track. There is a steelhead run here so I break out my fly rod. In the largest tidal pool at the river's mouth, salmon, steelhead trout, and mackerel leap, and harbor seals roll. I cast among them until dusk but catch nothing. We never see the white bear, but we know she is somewhere nearby.

The next morning, there she is, fishing the same pool I did with the same luck. We watch as she repeatedly waits on the tide line and leaps into the ocean only to catch nothing. It is a scene of simple elegance: On a slate-colored shoreline, perched on a dark ocean, walks the small white bear. The bear appears young, probably female, with a relatively small head on a body too large for an adolescent black bear. She is already fat, early in this river's season of sea-run fish. A slight reddish-brown yoke along the back of her neck runs halfway down her spine—possibly the result of foraging in streams rich in humic acids. Her mouth is open, she seems relaxed and preoccupied with searching for food, though this is likely "displacement behavior," a response inappropriate to the stimulus of our boat floating just offshore.

The lovely animal picks her way across the mouth of the river, where a fan of low waterfalls cascades into the ocean. She checks each pool and dives into the largest, submerging in the froth. After emerging, she continues along the shoreline. We watch as she stops to chew a clump of blue mussels and then looks up at us, seaweed hanging out of her mouth.

Among the Kitasoo/Xai'xais and Gitga'at Nations, the White Bear People were believed to be reminders left by Raven of the time when the land was white and covered with ice and snow. Raven set an island aside for the White Bear People. There, on the shores of Princess Royal, the White Bear People were meant to live in perpetuity.

I admit to having been prepared to resist both the legend and the appeal of the white Kermode bear—like a bad ad for Weyerhaeuser. But then I saw one, on its own terms. The presence of this vulnerable animal shattered my anthropomorphic prejudices.

A Kermode bear, as spirit bears are also
called, fishes for salmon in the Great Bear
Rainforest, British Columbia.
IAN MCALLISTER

TIGER TALES

Beyond the wing of the Aeroflot twin-engine plane unfolds a tapestry of green tundra and mottled muskeg, the wetlands sliced into crescents by dark arcs of old river channels. Timbered strips of spruce and fir fringe these waterways. A village of perhaps a couple hundred ethnic Russian and native Udege people looms in the crook of a broad bend of the river, now receding from the high flows of spring melt-off to expose wide sandbars and islands of willow. The little town is the first human sign on the land in over a hundred miles. Up ahead lies a range of low mountains, the summits traced by lines of snow cornices marking the rounded, windswept ridges. Beyond these hills, at the southeastern edge of the former Soviet Union, lies the Sea of Japan, where we plan to scout out a section of coast for a kayak trip.

It is late spring of 1992, just months after the fall of the Soviet Union and the emergence of the new independent Russian state.

Previous spread: An Amur, or Siberian, tiger, *Panthera tigris altaica*, near the Amur River in the Khabarovsk Territory in the Russian Far East. VLADIMIR FILONOV

On board this flying boxcar are many military men, a few Native families, a number of young men in leather jackets, and my companions, Jib Ellison and Doug Tompkins. Jib runs commercial river trips in Siberia and Central Asia. This hastily organized expedition is a buddy trip; the three of us merely the advance party. Our friends Yvon Chouinard and Rick Ridgeway are due to show up with Tom Brokaw in about a week. These men call themselves the "Do Boys" because, despite demanding professional lives, they get together about once a year and do things in the outdoors, like climb mountains or run rivers.

Chouinard and Tompkins know each other from the early sixties in California where they both surfed and climbed, and where Tompkins, at twenty-one, started a mountaineering company called The North Face, and later, Esprit. Tompkins, now retired from commercial enterprise, buys up national park–sized forests in order to preserve them. Chouinard founded Chouinard Equipment, and then Patagonia, Inc. Chouinard still runs Patagonia. Jib is a green entrepreneur. Together with Ridgeway, they are among the top outdoor clothing and equipment designers in the world and, even at the average age of almost sixty, these friends are considered among America's best mountaineers and kayakers, having climbed and paddled on seven continents.

While their name, the Do Boys, is derived from bad Japanese journalism and an inside joke, the trips these men take are serious, sometimes epic, and all the more so considering their busy lives.

Ridgeway met Brokaw on the *Today* show in 1982 after Rick had successfully climbed K2, the second-highest mountain in the world. After the show, Tom confessed that it had always been a dream of his to climb, and so the two of them joined Yvon Chouinard in Wyoming to scale the Grand Teton and Mount Moran. Later, the three of them teamed up with Doug Tompkins

CHAPTER 10

to climb Mount Rainier in Washington, reaching the summit in a whiteout.

Taking a comfortable trip with a group of strangers or herd of ecotourists to a scenic or interesting place was unacceptable for this group of men. Most of the Do Boys had passed the point of life where notions of recreation and mere curiosity about the exotic were sufficient justification to propel an adventure.

In my case, a strong preference for freedom of travel in wild places and an opportunity for solitude had limited my range. Ridgeway, Chouinard, and I had traveled and camped together on a desert island in Mexico, and Tompkins and I had flown parts of wild British Columbia looking for intact watersheds and kayaked in the Queen Charlottes. Later, Rick, Doug, and I had joined up in the wilds of Canada for a polar bear and beluga expedition, but—in contrast with my globe-rambling pals—I'd barely left North America in nearly twenty years.

Then, in 1989, my friend Ed Abbey died, and I had a wake-up call. I realized then that I, too, wasn't going to be around forever so I'd better take my walks and trips while I still could. Now in my fifties, I have returned to Asia, for the first time since my days as a Green Beret medic in Vietnam, to see the salmon rivers at the edge of Siberia, maybe follow tiger tracks along the Sea of Japan, and then head to the Himalaya to look for a snow leopard.

The idea of going to southeastern Russia surfaced during a fishing trip in Montana. Famed attorney Gerry Spence, Chouinard's neighbor and godfather of Yvon's son, Fletcher, was discussing the best places left on Earth to see wild tigers with Peter Matthiessen. Since it was my fishing hole and I was interested, I felt comfortable eavesdropping; I had seen tiger tracks numerous times in the Vietnam highlands, but my military-subsidized misadventures were nothing compared to the far-ranging travels of Peter and Gerry. The enduring vision that

196

The team takes a break on the Bikin
River, Russian Far East, 1992. Left to right:
Yvon Chouinard, Doug Tompkins, Jib
Ellison, Tom Brokaw, and Doug Peacock.
RICK RIDGEWAY

An Amur tiger races over the snow.
Russian Far East. SMITH ARCHIVE/
ALAMY

emerged from this exchange was that of a Siberian tiger walking a winter beach on the Pacific Ocean—the quintessence of wild tigerdom.

It turned out that subliminal image had already been envisioned. Another climber friend, Jack Turner, had given me a rare edition of a remarkable book called *Dersu the Trapper*, written by a young Russian geographer, V.K. Arseniev, who made three expeditions to the Primorsky Krai, or Maritime Province, between 1902 and 1907. Dersu was his guide and the spirit of *amba*, the local tribe's name for tiger, permeates this wonderful account of exploration in these virgin forests.

So, after several false starts trying to find a wild trip in the Russian Far East, Yvon called with news that Dr. Maurice Hornocker had invited him to fly fish the rivers draining the Sikhote-Alin mountains, where Hornocker was conducting a Siberian tiger study. And we all jumped on it.

Dr. Hornocker had set up the Siberian Tiger project in 1992 to save the last of the world's largest cats because by 1989, the Siberian, or Amur, tiger was effectively extinct in China and the two Koreas, with perhaps only a few hundred great cats remaining in the Russian Far East.

The Amur tiger is but one of nine geographical races, or subspecies, of this magnificent animal, three of which vanished in the 1900s. Only the Amur, Sumatran, Indochinese, South China, Malayan, and Indian survive. Just the Indian and, hopefully, the Amur (or Siberian) populations are given much hope of surviving into the near future.

Back in 1936, only about fifty Amur tigers were believed to exist—too few, many thought, for the genetic variation necessary for longtime survival. During and after World War II, when potential poachers were busy fighting Germans, the great cat made a comeback. By the mid-1980s, some 250 adults were believed to live in the wild. But with the implosion of the Soviet Union, international poaching hit the Russian Far East with a vengeance and an estimated third of the wild tiger population was decimated. A dead cat brings in thousands of dollars for tiger skins and bones; the bones are often ground up to use in medicine, and penises are used as an aphrodisiac and sold in Korea, China, Vietnam, Japan, and Taiwan.

On this relatively tame trip we also want to explore some wild country—a river or piece of coastline—using collapsible sea kayaks; we don't know where exactly because the political logistics of travel in the former Soviet Union are still complicated. The interests of these men are as eclectic as their backgrounds: Yvon wants to sample the fishing, Doug is looking for virgin timber to maybe try to buy up and preserve, and Tom is anticipating some travel with a few friends without the usual entourage of newspersons and political leaders.

Brokaw, in fact, considers his friendship with Ridgeway, Tompkins, and Chouinard a "wonderful result of climbing. Now I have lifelong friends who I am very fond of. We've shared a lot of adventures."

Jib is a student of the culture, and my own interest is skewed toward wild animals that sometimes kill and eat you—like tigers and bears.

Everyone wants to see this land, the largest forest on Earth, known by its Russian name, taiga, the greatest timber resource and wildlife habitat in the hemisphere. We'd like to know what the Russians plan to do with the taiga: set it aside as preserves, continue to protect it as native homelands, or sell it off to foreign logging companies.

What is perhaps most inviting about traveling with the Do Boys is less that they travel to exotic places for dangerous adventure than that they have genuine curiosity about the wide world, and all try, in their own remarkable ways, to beneficially affect its future.

Out the window, the slate-gray ocean glints in the east and the dark mass of Sakhalin Island hangs on the horizon. A huge fire has ravaged the forest; only ribbons of larch and birch along the creeks have survived the flames. The plane descends into the harbor of Sovetskaya Gavan, a natural anchorage littered with rusting ships and a gray necklace of dreary concrete buildings ringing the bay—the industrial clutter of the cities stands in stark contrast to the beauty of the countryside.

Though I had told my friends I was going to the southeastern edge of Siberia, no one here calls it that. This region is known as the Russian Far East. Elsewhere in Siberia the resources are gas, oil, coal, uranium, gold, and diamonds, but here it is timber that is the top export commodity. Siberia means the sleeping land, but with the collapse of much of the Soviet infrastructure, people are reeling, and the country is waking like a cranky grizzly rudely roused from his den by an avalanche in late February. Despite the material bleakness of the cities, the country feels a lot like Alaska did when oil was discovered there; Siberia and the Russian Far East are on the brink of a boom. An early riser could get rich.

In minutes, we land and collect our backpacks, boat bags, and folding kayaks. We wait for our ride in what might be a bar; there are dusty bottles of mystery booze lined up on a grimy counter. Through the window I can see a junkyard of buses and plane wings.

Travel in the former Soviet Union is difficult. It is very hard to get off by yourself. Here, someone is always officially accountable for your safety; the notion of being responsible for one's own ass is unknown. It is true that the old bureaucratic inflexibility was perhaps beginning to unravel, but this relaxation of the rules had yet to drift out to eastern Siberia. On the other hand, there is a comfortable anarchy here and everything is cheap. To get to Sovetskaya Gavan, we had simply paid five bucks to change a visa and hopped on an airplane.

The one constant that remains is the soul of Russia; long after the scenes of dreary city life and funeral lines of bureaucrats examining your papers fade from memory, you recall the hearts and hospitality of the people.

We ask if we can go into the Botcha and have a look. A Russian biologist named Valera befriends us. A round of negotiations begins. The captain of the only "available" boat—though there are hundreds in the harbor—wants an arm and a leg to take us down there. Valera, whom I immediately take a liking to, takes charge and gets the price down to $90.

Valera tells us about the threatened Botcha valley, how wild and rich it is and how perhaps as many as seven Siberian tigers have ranges that include parts of the drainage.

"Maybe, if we like it, we'll buy it," says Doug Tompkins, introducing the alien notion of private ownership and the foreign idea of buying the land in order to save it.

The silence is followed by nervous laughter. This is a difficult concept to grasp for our Russian friends.

"Who owns this land and how much would they sell it for per hectare?" continues Doug. He used this strategy successfully in Chile where he outbid the timber companies and bought up thousands of hectares of forest.

Though the Russians have not yet entered the era where private citizens and groups can own land, they are moving toward it. Tompkins is the ultimate can-do guy, and he is, if necessary, prepared to take on the devastation of the world's forests single-handedly. The man loves forests. When he finds one he likes, he buys it. Instead of writing his representative, he just writes a check. Doug owns a number of forests, and some of them are bigger than some national parks. Down in South America, he bought one complete with glaciers, a fjord, and his own active volcano. He doesn't do anything to them; he just wants to protect them from industrial destruction. If Native or subsistence people live there, he simply pencils them into the deed with a grandfather clause.

The next morning, Valera and we three Americans board the sixty-foot boat to Kopii, a small village on the way to Botcha. Perhaps thirty Russians live there, along with fifty dogs of vague husky descent, most of them puppies. The few passengers debark there and that gives us room to break out our folding kayaks for assembly. Jib and Doug are sharing a two-person Klepper; I have a new Feathercraft model borrowed from Brokaw. We put these boats together in time for a quick float just before dark. We want to be ready for the Botcha.

Later, we are dieseling south on the big boat when we flag down a crab boat to see if we can buy some fresh crab. Valera does the talking and the captain of the crabber sends for a man who comes out with an armload of perhaps fifty pounds of huge, fresh, boiled Kamchatka crabs—all he can carry. I ask Jib to find out how much we owe, and during the translation we get another enormous load of crabs. We offer to trade cigarettes, but the Russians respond with a twenty-kilo block of frozen crabmeat. The crew of the crab ship, men who make less than $2 a day, refuse to be paid; the crabs are a gift. Finally, they accept tiny pins from America as souvenirs and a drink of vodka.

We put in at the village of Grossevichi at the mouth of the Botcha. The game warden here is a hunter named Gorbachev who will be both our host and guide. Gorbi is two days from forty-eight, tall and very muscular, like many mature Russian men on the frontier. Only Gorbachev and two other families live here, although there is a twenty-man military detachment. Everywhere, tiny plots of potatoes are planted to ward off the hunger of winter; there are gardens, smoked fish, salted Chinese garlic, wild greens, moose meat in the cold box, and barrels of smelt.

I walk out to the yard along the ocean where there is a clothesline. Pinned to the line are hundreds of seven-inch-long fish drying in the late-spring sunlight. These smelt, I think, are similar to the eulachon, or candlefish, of British Columbia, so rich in oil that they burn like a wick when dried.

Gorbachev's log house is hot but comfortable; the woodstove to boil tea water also heats the place. Tomorrow, he says, we will go up the Botcha. Doug and Jib sack out; I go fishing with Gorbi, Valera, and two soldiers. A light rain falls as we motor upstream in the long, flat-bottomed boat. On the way up, we pass mergansers, dippers, osprey, and fish eagles. Purple herons lift off the bend of the river ahead. Gorbi supplies me with a short, stiff rod—the type that my family back in Michigan used to call "meat-rods"—and shows me how and where to flip the crudely hammered homemade lure. On his first cast, Gorbi hooks and quickly reels in a two-pound char, a fish like our Dolly Varden or brook trout. Before long, all three Russians are hauling in char while I am still fooling with the ancient reel. Gorbi and one of the men each land a silver salmon, about six pounds. Finally, I cast well out into the current, let the lure swing below me, and start a retrieve: a three-pound char immediately hits. The fish are pulled in businesslike with little notion of sport. Even the tiny char are kept, tossed in the boat. These men are fishing for food. A pounding rain nails our skiff going back downstream and we squint into the downpour. In the driving rain, Valera yells out to me and points out a pair of chestnut-winged Mandarin ducks roosting on a gravel bar.

Back at Gorbi's cabin, Doug and Jib are up. A few of Gorbi's friends sit around a long table with Doug at the far end and me at the head. The rounds begin with pounding down shots of rotgut vodka and toasting anything, and I realize Tompkins has set me up. Since everyone is watching me, I can't get out of it, though I am sick to death of vodka after the past few days of getting to know these wonderful Russians. Meanwhile, Tompkins pours the contents of his glass into the planter he has conveniently chosen to sit next to. Doug proposes yet another toast from the end of the table: "Screw Hyundai!" He does this five more times, five more big shots of vodka, which he dumps out when no one is looking. I pray he doesn't kill the plant, and hope I don't offend my new friends by puking on the table. Tompkins has a big, shit-eating grin on his face.

The next morning, two flat-bottomed riverboats take the three of us with our kayaks up the Botcha. I shake off my hangover; it's a pleasure to get back into the country. We stop at a sledge trail to walk up into the taiga. The cottonwood, alder, and birch of the river bottom gives way to towering larch, fir, spruce, and a sprinkling of Korean pine trees. This is where Weyerhaeuser wants to clear-cut. In the Russian Far East, there are two types of forest that grade into each other: to our south lies a hardwood forest of oak and Korean pine, and to the north, beginning here on the Botcha, is the boreal forest of spruce, fir, larch, and, where there has been a forest fire, birch.

In the mud are the prints of many moose, Asian wild dog (dhole), sika deer, brown bear, lynx, and mink; this forest supports an amazing amount of wildlife. No sign of tiger, though I know they live here. The willow is just budding here in the northern Sikhote-Alin. The pitted heads of black morel mushrooms pop out from under a charred log; I gather a batch for dinner.

The Russians go back to the village, leaving us alone, which they are reluctant to do; our desire to be on our own makes them uncomfortable. This is less a form of suspicion than a legacy of their bureaucratic culture born of a swaddled cradleboard during infancy. I hook and beach a seven-pound salmon for dinner and we make camp on the edge of a wedge of tundra a quarter mile wide and long, the only open ground for miles along the river. Up on the bank, a game trail leads through the dwarf willow with tracks of moose and the scat of bear.

I pitch my tent out of sight of Jib and Doug, savoring a moment of precious solitude, listening to the calls of ravens, cuckoos, and other unfamiliar birds echoing in the still forest. More kinds of mammal species live in these boreal woods than any place I've ever traveled. A tremendous amount of uninhabited land lies deeper in the taiga. This reserve is unlike American parks with our administrators and wilderness visitors; nobody's out here. The Russians leave these lands to fend for themselves, protected by remoteness. The wild corner of my soul is envious.

I imagine sneaking off by myself and illegally exploring the reserve—camping alone with the tigers and bears. Solitude in wilderness is the easiest escape from the prison of culture and self-importance. It's there just out of reach; I can almost smell it.

Later, we build a fire of wet alder and larch, carefully lighting the inner bark of birch to slowly dry the spruce twigs until the branches catch fire. Finally, I stuff the salmon with mushrooms and dust the exterior with Cavender's Greek Seasoning. I wrap the fish in foil and slowly bake it over a thin layer of alder coals. The three of us drift off in different directions to savor this wild forest. By the time we return to camp, the salmon is perfectly cooked.

Wild dogs bark and yowl up and down the river. We try to stoke up the campfire. Across the stretch of tundra, I catch sight of what looks like a large tabby cat against the tree line. The shapes of dhole dance in the shadows. An amazing menagerie of carnivores roams the taiga, mammals I have never seen before, like raccoon dogs and the tabby cat. The only image missing in this primordial landscape is a 450-pound tiger roaming the heather.

As recently as the nineteenth century, the Siberian tiger was common in northeastern China, Siberia, and the Korean peninsula, and ranged west as far as Mongolia and Lake Baikal. Now the heart of the Amur tiger range lies in the Sikhote-Alin, the

The Bikin River winds through the Bikin
National Park, one of Russia's largest, in
the north of Primorsky Krai in the Russian
Far East. YURI SMITYUK\TASS VIA
GETTY IMAGES

Bikin River, and up here in the Botcha, at the northern limit of surviving tigers.

We squat around the poorly burning alder fire. I tell my friends about burying my friend Ed Abbey in a lovely, illegal grave deep in the desert. We speak of mortality, of dreams.

In the morning, we pack the kayaks and head downstream, dawdling, gawking at ducks and woodpeckers, checking the sandbars for animal tracks—wishing the trip would take a week instead of the three hours that it does. This part of the Botcha isn't quite big enough for the Do Boys.

Our Russian friends have accommodated our desires as best they could under their own system of reserves; we got to sample the Botcha. But I don't want to just write notes about this magnificent country; I want to penetrate its wilderness, chew on its flora, and spend weeks on a quest for a Siberian tiger.

Back in Sovetskaya Gavan, we are too late to catch the last plane out. The hotel costs only about $2 and comes with hot running water, a rarity. I take two showers and wash my clothes. The three of us have dinner in the empty hotel lobby with a Russian rock band playing very loud, very bad music through a blown speaker. A tabby cat sprawls out on the dance floor and an old crone from the street dances around the cat until the hotel manager throws them both out. On her way out the door, the woman grabs our table and shouts demands at Jib. Maybe she wants a drink. I pour two big glasses of vodka, push one across the table, and toast the old woman.

"Za vashe zdorovie." Cheers.

We fly back to Khabarovsk, the far eastern capital of Siberia, to meet our friends. Outside the airport, crowded circles of Chinese and Korean businessmen wheel and deal, buying up newly arrived merchandise. Finally, we find Chouinard, Ridgeway, and Brokaw standing with the big-cat biologist Maurice Hornocker. Dr. Hornocker, famous for his research on mountain lions in

Idaho and New Mexico, is undertaking a study of Siberian tigers, a joint venture with several Russian and American scientists. The biologist's first choice for a study area was a scientific reserve near Terney, about three hundred miles southeast of here on the coast; the second choice was the remote upper Bikin River, where tigers, bears, and other animals must share the habitat with Native peoples. We must find a way to see these places.

Our plane can't fly because of poor weather so we're stuck for the night. In Khabarovsk's best restaurant, a Japanese joint venture, young Russian hustlers come to the table peddling ivory, claiming the fresh tusk is prehistoric mammoth. I go with Brokaw into the saloon for a nightcap. Ridgeway joins us at the bar and takes a seat between me and a comely, if heavily made-up, young Russian woman who immediately pulls her blouse down off both shoulders and tells Rick in perfect English that she comes here each night to meet Americans. We down our vodka and retreat outside. Along the muddy sides of dilapidated sidewalks, near the broken pipelines, I read the sign in the dirt: deep, oval tracks of many stylish high-heeled shoes that, nonetheless, must take the sloppy walk each day to work or market. Almost everyone over twenty has gold teeth, and pretty girls spit in the street. There is no hot water because the city is hoarding its limited stores of natural gas for the winter cold.

Though this land is lovely, even bountiful, there remains the unmistakable impression that the industrial cornerstone of the cities could collapse at any time. Yvon and Doug discuss this situation.

"Nothing works, everything is broken."

"There is no sense of quality."

"The people are beaten and hopeless."

"The youth are too far gone to turn things around."

Ridgeway and Ellison tell of their American friend who spent a year living in Siberia like a Russian. He lived in a city dependent on airplanes for resupply. During the winter, no amount of money could buy food; you needed coupons issued by the government to Russian citizens only. He survived on imported canned seaweed from Japan, which the Russians despised and wouldn't eat. To this day his greatest fear—and this is no timid, sedentary man—is the utter helplessness of starving to death in a winter city dependent on Aeroflot.

Since quality and workmanship seem poor, natural resources such as timber appear to be the quick fix, the prime candidate for export. For my worldly companions and me, this is a frightening prognosis.

The plane we have chartered to Terney flies over the Bikin River Valley, one of the biggest drainages in the Russian Far East, homeland of native Udege people who hunt and trap there. The upper regions of the watershed are pristine, wild, and teeming with wildlife; including, perhaps, a fifth of the remaining tigers in the Russian Far East.

The Siberian, or Amur, tiger is properly known as *Panthera tigris altaica*; the Amur tiger's historic range included northern Korea and northeastern China—an ecological zone with flora typified by the big five-needle pine, the Korean cedar. No one knows how many tigers inhabit this range; though, as evidenced by the annual reported kills of 120 to 150 at the turn of the century, it was many more than today. By the 1940s, the habitat was fragmented and population segments isolated; the hunting and taking of live cubs (invariably resulting in the death of the mother tiger and the rest of the litter) for zoos had greatly reduced the population. In 1947, the hunting of tigers was banned but the capture of tiger cubs for zoos continued. The number of tigers in the entire Russian Far East had plummeted to a low of a few dozen animals. But by 1959, 90 to 100 animals were estimated for the Far East. And by 1970, Russian Amur tigers had increased to 150 or so, although the isolated Chinese and Korean populations had declined to only a few dozen.

Dr. Hornocker's three-year study is a joint project with the Hornocker Wildlife Institute and three full-time Russian scientists. Maurice believes the well-being of big carnivores like tigers and bears is indicative of the health of the entire ecosystem; through this work, they hope to "create an understanding of man's place in the world's fragile ecological structure and his responsibility to it."

Maurice must attend to duties elsewhere in the reserve. A truck carries us south to the headquarters of the team that is studying tigers. A colleague of Hornocker's, the on-site US scientist Dr. Dale Miquelle from Massachusetts, briefs us on the study and takes us on a walk down to the bay. The biologists have decided they must radio-collar a number of tigers in order to figure out their ranges and movements. Progress has been slow; the tigers are hard to catch. They have only been able to catch one animal, a young female. The pits favored by the Russians didn't work. The American biologists happened to have brought along a few leg snares and one worked. They named the tiger Olga. They tranquilized her and took a small sample of tissue. She weighed in at 190 pounds. Dale placed the tissue sample in a canister packed with dry ice and sent it back to his colleagues in America, Howard and Kathy Quigley, for DNA analysis. The canister was returned to Miquelle, airfreight and packed again with dry ice, this time containing a pint of Ben & Jerry's ice cream.

Not all is well in the Sikhote-Alin Biosphere Reserve. Dr. Miquelle and his Russian colleagues know of six tiger skins for sale in nearby towns. When a Korean fur trader heard that Dale was interested in tigers, he tried to sell Miquelle a skin.

On the coarse upper beach of the bay we find the tracks of the young female tiger that had walked south the morning before. Brokaw and I find the much larger tracks of a male tiger that

Siberian tiger skin recovered from poachers in Primorsky Krai, Russian Far East.
STEVE MORGAN/GREENPEACE

passed that way a week or so ago. I feel a tingling up my spine as I remember that Dersu and Arseniev walked this beach. An ancient connection draws me closer to Dersu's world; inspiration from literature can propel actual adventure trips halfway around the world.

The live oak forests of southeastern Ussuriland, a large maritime province, are evocative of what I imagine the great chestnut forests of the eastern United States once were. The woodlands are lovely, open and dappled with light. Musk deer, roe deer, sika deer (a kind of white-tailed deer), elk, moose, boar, and bear share the habitat with tigers, leopards, and numerous smaller carnivores. The tigers feed on boar and deer. The wild boar, like the smaller javelina of my own Southwest, are easy to stalk and sneak up on, though fiercely tusked and tough to kill. The big five-needle Korean pines here are called cedar. They produce big cones and sweet pine nuts preferred by boar and bear. The resinous wood of the pine makes for easy fire starting in even the wettest weather.

In order to visit the countryside, we are told it is necessary to secure a permit from the bureau of tourism. We return to Terney where the director of tourism offers us a river trip using our own kayaks for only $2,100.

"A truck and motorboat will accompany you at all times," he says.

This is not exactly what we had in mind. I stare out the window of what, until recently, used to be the Communist Party building; an attractive girl is walking her cow down the street.

"This is banditry," says Brokaw, who along with Jib has acquired the unsolicited job of group diplomat.

We are getting nowhere. Jib stands up and announces, "We're out of here, we are going home."

The best thing about this bunch of Americans is that they are good sports, roll with the punches, and there is no whining.

By chance, we meet a biologist on loan from the Pacific Geographical Institute in Vladivostok, Dimitri Pikunov, a fifty-three-year-old PhD who has lived in the Bikin to study bears and tigers. He knows we are interested in preserving wildlands. His greatest personal accomplishment, he tells us, was in helping establish a Native People's Reserve in the Bikin for the subsistence Udege people. The Bikin River country, he argues, is "the most beautiful, most pristine of all."

"You must see it," he says. "Hyundai wants to cut it all down and Moscow will cave into them."

The die is cast. We decide to ignore the warnings that we must get permission from the KGB to travel, and try to hire or bribe a helicopter pilot on our own to fly us and our kayaks into the headwaters of the Bikin River. It can be done, we hear.

———

We are flying. Our map shows the Zeva River, the middle tributary of the Bikin River, unfurling counterclockwise, flowing through eroded volcanic hills and cliffs of columnar basalt, finally hooking into the Bikin. That's where we want to go.

Yvon and I look out the open window of the big military-style Aeroflot helicopter; Rick has opened the port in order to take some photographs for a magazine assignment he and I have to help pay expenses. As our only map of the area is passed to me, I stupidly grab it in front of the window. In a heartbeat, half the map—the half that shows the Zeva and all the country we plan on kayaking—rips off and is sucked out the window. We are now mapless and I wonder what my carelessness foreshadows. Much later, Brokaw will make me pay heavily, in hilarious prose, for my blunder. Fortunately, rivers tend to run in one direction.

I am awe-struck by the expanse of trees and pristine habitat below. The big oaks and pine slowly give way to smaller trees, the transition to the boreal forest.

"The forest looks like it's kinda crapped out," says Tompkins.

I throw Doug a sniggering comment on the chauvinism of big-tree guys and he laughs. The mood is good.

For 150 miles, only the lightest hand of humans shows upon the land; the entire taiga remains uncut. This vast expanse of dark green fir, spruce, and larch is streaked and traced by the lighter greens of cottonwood and alder growing along the river bottoms and the apple-green tops of huge live oaks running along the ridges: the enormous scale of this virgin forest takes the breath away. West of Svetlaya, however, the Korean giant Hyundai has been operating for a year and many thousands of hectares of timberland are clear-cut.

I check off the list of trees: The forest is a mix of broadleaf and conifer, with more conifers at higher elevations and more broadleaf in the lower valleys. The most common species are the Korean pine and needle fir at the lowest elevations and coastlines. Spruce and Manchurian fir are common from seven hundred to fourteen hundred meters in elevation. Other tree species include Mongolian oak, birch, aspen, and, especially to the north, larch. If you are familiar with the boreal forests of North America, none of this will surprise you; it's just an incredible amount of vegetative diversity crammed into a relatively small region.

Also, the Russian Far East is the only place in the world where tigers, brown bears, and leopards coexist. This region contains some of the last habitat of the Blakiston's fish owl, the world's largest owl.

An hour or so later, south of the high tableland, the chopper banks west toward the headwaters of the Bikin River and into the watershed of the Zeva, a major tributary looping through the wooded hill country of the Ussuri uplands in broad, meandering bends interrupted by big rocks and small rapids. We have not seen a road or human dwelling since the Hyundai clear-cuts.

A mother and her yearling stand to see
and smell better. The Russian Far East
is the only place where brown bears,
panthers, and tigers occupy the same habitat. BEAR CONSERVATION/CREATIVE
COMMONS LICENSE

Suddenly the big chopper wheels over and drops into the river valley just above the tops of spruce and fir trees. Ahead, a blue haze of woodsmoke billows up from a clearing in the taiga. A low log cabin and two huts come into view—a tiny Udege settlement.

We kick our considerable baggage out of the hovering chopper door, jump down onto the soggy tundra, and stand clear of the rotor blast. Jib slaps a roll of rubles into the pilot's hand for his trouble and for the unscheduled touchdown; the crew will split the bounty tonight back in Vladivostok. We give them a thumbs-up and the huge helicopter lifts off. We are left alone on the taiga.

The sound of the helicopter fades and the songs of thrushes, nuthatches, and cuckoos rise from the forest canopy. Walking behind a small storage hut of sticks and small logs to take a leak, I come face-to-face with the fresh hide of a large bear species I have not seen before. The skin has a white collar of fur across its brown chest and the claws are impressive—an *Ursus thibetanus*, or Asiatic black bear. Its bloody skull grins nearby on a stump overlooking the river. These people are hunters and trappers.

This Asiatic black bear is the most common bear here, but it is not the only one. Asian brown bear, *Ursus arctos*—the same species as our grizzly bear—also occupy these forests and steppes. Dimitri has told me that the *Ursus arctos* of the Bikin region grow big, a thousand pounds and more, as big as the coastal brown bear of Alaska. The difference between the European or Asian brown bear and the American grizzly is mostly one of behavior that resulted from the grizzly having further evolved on the open tundra of Alaska where the only defense—for a mother bear defending her cubs from wolves, other bears, and several now-extinct Pleistocene carnivores—was a good offense. Thus, the grizzly bear is considered much more aggressive than the Asian brown bear, from whom they are direct descendants. But all these bears can be dangerous to humans.

CHAPTER 10

A green-alder fire burns next to a smoking shed where a row of copper-colored fish hangs from a clothesline. I glance inside the cabin. All is brown. Amber sunlight filters through the window into the smoky haze of the room. All wood surfaces wear a bronze patina of decades of woodsmoke. A round-faced woman with strong Asian features sits silently at the table.

The Udege boat ferries our gear across to a gravel bar where we can set up camp for the night and assemble our kayaks. A man called Valentine poles the long flat-bottomed craft across the stiff current. Halfway across the river, in a swirl of roily water, I look straight down into the face of a moose; this disturbing image causes me a moment of confusion. Then, as the boat swings around the eddy, I see that the entire carcass is tethered to a big alder by a rope. It's only an Udege cold-storage system.

We set up our tents, build a fire for a pot of tea, and finish putting together the kayaks. Just at dusk, the Udege men pole across the river with a big stew bowl of moose liver and sirloin. Tom breaks out a fifth of very good Scotch whiskey, pours big shots for all, and we slam them down Russian-style.

"The Udege will fight with guns," a tall Udege answers when I ask him about the prospect of Hyundai or other timber giants coming into their country to log. I wonder about folk for whom resistance is lived as chunks of daily life, especially in a place like this, haunted by the ghosts of countless generations of hunters and warriors—a land prowled by giant cats and bears.

Dimitri explains that we have over 125 miles of river to cover in six days before we hit a road where we hope to hire a truck to haul us to the Trans-Siberian Railway. Apparently, Dimi has some plan and schedule in mind, but it's too complicated to translate. The best fishing, he adds, is in the upper sections of the river, so we should use our fly rods tomorrow. Two days downstream, adds Dimi, is a bad rapid.

Yvon and Rick talk quietly to Tom, giving him kayaking advice.

"It's like a party," says Ridgeway, "you don't want to be first and you don't want to be last."

If you are first in line, they explain, there will be no one downstream to pick you up or grab your floating gear. Yvon tells a story to show the possible consequences of being last in a line of kayakers paddling down a wild river: Bob McDougall, an employee of Patagonia, the company Chouinard started, was kayaking the Grand Canyon of the Stikine River in southeastern Alaska, a river with the most challenging whitewater in North America. He was the last coming down the narrow, deep canyon and got caught in a suckhole rapid. He bailed out of his kayak, which along with his gear never came up. He swam to the nearest vertical wall and managed to rock climb the sheer (5.7 climbing rating) wall up to the forest. His companions couldn't paddle back upstream to help him. Wearing only his shorts and no shoes, he walked for three days to Telegraph Creek.

In the morning, the good weather appears to have stabilized; not a single cloud breaks the clear expanse of blue sky beyond the deep green of the fully leafed cottonwood. We heat coffee and tea water over a fire of willow twigs, spend an hour packing all our gear in the compartments of the kayaks, and finally push off at about ten in the morning. It's good to finally be on the water with a long run of river ahead.

The river seems halfway between the streams of my Michigan boyhood and the Montana rivers I've fished ever since—a bit of color and a few rocks and logjams, but mostly a gentle float. The easiest fish to catch on flies is the lenok; we hear they run to ten pounds, though they average only a couple of pounds for us. They look like trout with broad, fat lips. There are also the fabled taimen, up to two hundred pounds, that rise to lemmings during their rodent migrations. We don't know much about them; only Yvon, the most resourceful and innovative fly fisherman I know, gets any—a few small ones on streamers. We catch some grayling on streamers and nymphs. Wagtails are nesting in the willows along the river's edge. The long day winds down.

Though four of our group are among the top ten whitewater kayakers in the world, there is no competition on this easy river. What unspoken struggle there is involves Brokaw and me for "worst" in paddling skill. Although I have spent a tame week or two in sea kayaks and have been down many rivers in rafts, canoes, or drift boats, I have the least experience in river kayaking. Brokaw has the advantage of having been taught the Eskimo roll by Yvon in Wyoming, while I haven't even read that chapter yet.

We have a cup of tea before entering the rapids Dimitri has told us about. I follow Yvon through; it isn't bad at all.

Chouinard stops to fish and I go ahead. I delight in dodging the rocks and running through modest standing waves in minor rapids. I pass Tom, who is next to shore pumping out his kayak. After successfully getting through the little rapids, he was fooling with his spray skirt when a low alder branch swept him out of his cockpit. I paddle past, and then swing into a back eddy to give assistance. But it isn't necessary; he is merely wet.

I paddle on feeling a bit superior; I enjoy being the lead boat, rounding each bend of river with a fresh sense of anticipation and discovery. Along the shaded bank, I smell the fragrance of dogwood and rose hips. For the next hour I dodge boulders and negotiate small rapids; I feel like an old hand in the kayak business. Three big rocks loom ahead. I miss the first two but read the river wrong and fight the current on the third and lose. The current pushes me up on the rock and I dump. Fortunately, the water is only waist-deep and I quickly haul the water-filled craft to shore and pour all but about a hundred pounds of water out

The crew kayaking the Bikin River in
the Russian Far East, 1992. Tom and
Doug vie for worst kayaking skills.
RICK RIDGEWAY

of the kayak. I climb back in just in time as Yvon comes into view. I push off and paddle away as if nothing has happened, hoping I haven't been seen. The cockiness has disappeared. There is no arrogance in my stroke; paddling the water-laden craft is ponderous.

At the confluence of Zeva and Bikin, I pause in an eddy and bail out the remaining hundred pounds of water with my canteen cup. Rick and Tom join me, and we wait for Dimitri.

We now move rapidly with the current; the river is muscular with the sinewy body of a python. A gray kestrel streaks across it, and back in the forest I hear parrot-like calls. On the bank near our last campsite was the track of a huge brown bear—as big as any track I have seen. We haven't seen many animals out and about during daylight hours. Though this is some of the very best Siberian tiger country, we have yet to see a big-cat track here. As I paddle around each bend of the river, I expect to see the red flash of a tiger or the brown bulk of a bear. Later in the days, we sometimes spot deer, but during the day, the weather has been very warm and clear—too hot for big mammals.

The next day we pause at the confluence of a major tributary. Dimi hikes upstream to the Udege village. I beach my kayak on a bar at the junction of the two rivers and roll-cast a small stonefly nymph. I catch four grayling and turn a big lenok.

Flatboats arrive and we are motored back upstream to the village. Because we are behind the schedule that apparently only Dimitri knows, we must use motorboats to get down to the Amba River. We reluctantly disassemble and pack up the kayaks. The thirty or so people here are both Udege and Russian. Later, they stoke up a *banya*, the traditional bath; there is only room for three of us at a time in the sweathouse. By the time it is my turn, Rick, Tom, and Yvon stand steaming away in the middle of the cold river, naked as newts. In the bath, Dimitri gently whips my back with leafed branches of birch until I can take the steam no longer. I dive into the cold river. From Dimitri, Jib translates the phrase for this brisk experience: "Your balls come out your ears."

Dimi insists we visit an old gold mine. The Udege and other locals fear the government, or some big foreign company, will come back, strip-mine the mountain for its placer gold, and pollute their river. The light is flat, the scene cluttered, and photographer Ridgeway is beginning to lose his sense of humor. Dimitri will not take no for an answer: "This is a bad place," he says. "You should take some pictures."

The morning is buggy and Dimitri is swearing a lot, using something like the F-word in every other sentence. Jib explains that the exact translation is "penis." That is, "Get your penis muddy boots out of my penis kayak." Jib says that the ultimate use of this word is used to herald impending doom: "A dark sky of penises is gathering."

The boatmen are also cranky today. Dimitri is nervous; there is some question about our permission to be here or to travel in the reserve, and he could be responsible—something about the KGB. Meanwhile, a cloud of phalluses in the shape of a thunderhead gathers just to our north. Rumbles of thunder roll through the forest and bolts of lightning strike the range of hills north of us. The tall Udege in the bow of the lead boat is feuding with the other boatman when the motor conks out. The craft hits a big cottonwood log jutting out from the bank, overturns, and the current pins it against the big trunk. The Udege men jump to safety on the cottonwood log.

"That boat's history," says Tompkins, as we fish floating bundles out of the river downstream. We stop on a sandbar, build a fire, and erect tents, but the storm misses us. Somehow the Udege manage to cut the tree in half, losing a rifle and some gear, but recovering the invaluable boat and motor.

Downstream we put back in, but take a break before moving on. Tracks of brown bear, badger, and sable are printed in the mud. Tompkins and Chouinard sit quietly in the sunlight.

"I never dream like this at home," says Yvon.

We are all lost in our own thoughts for a minute, then Doug tells us about his dream, a recurring one, where he is floating down a huge river like the Congo. Suddenly, he looks at the face of his boatman who is transfixed "like a chicken staring at a cobra." In his dream, Doug turns around to see that the river suddenly narrows and disappears over a drop not unlike Niagara Falls.

"Better take a real big breath," Doug thinks, then, in his haunted dream, he covers his head with his arms as the boat disappears over the abyss. Underneath the water, all is foam, his arms are still wrapped around his head. He holds his breath as long as he can; after a long time, it occurs to him that he can breathe a little bit under the water.

Sitting along the Bikin River, no one laughs. It is sobering.

The only sound is the river and birdsong coming from the forest. The river dream troubles me; I almost drowned in a raging torrent last year during a canoeing accident. I don't share my private uneasiness with my world-class kayak friends. I need to see a tiger.

The boats drop us at a trapper's cabin Dimitri used in past years during his study of bears and tigers here. The Amba River bottom in late spring is hot and humid. I recall that Dersu came through here eighty years ago. Dimitri leads us on a hike several miles upriver. Shoulder-high cone fern and alder obstruct the vision. Moss and shelf fungus grow on logs and downfalls. During the winters of his bear study, Dimitri would ski along game trails, banging on cottonwood trunks with a heavy club, waking the Asian black bears that hibernated within the hollow trees. This is also prime tiger habitat. China lemon vine grows on the smaller trees, and cow parsnip and nettles make up the understory. Ticks hang off the low vegetation and we stop for a tick-check every fifteen minutes. This is our last day in the wilds; tonight, we move down to the big Udege village where we can hire a truck.

We climb a steep hill to a ridge. There is wild boar and black bear sign everywhere. Dimitri signals for us to be quiet. The crew is noisy, distracted, self-absorbed, talking loudly of industrial collapse and geopolitics.

Dimitri snaps at us to shut up. I can hear movement down the ridge.

Up ahead we hear the breathing sounds of big animals, either the huffing of bear or snorting of boar now invisibly running away. We blew it.

The world is only as big as we allow it to be. Wild places and animals pass on their secrets only if we listen. You need to pay attention. A touch of danger would help. You need to know you can die: a surprise rapid the size of Lava Falls; a bad stretch of black ice across an ice chute; a whiteout on a glacier; or a tiger, a leopard, a jaguar, or maybe a bear. But it's hard on our last day before the slow exit home. It's especially hard in a group; the social dynamics can drain you of vital curiosity and attentiveness. We got sloppy.

I take advantage of the disruption to split off by myself for a short time. Up the slope, Asiatic black bear have ripped branches off trees everywhere. I find daybeds of boar and bear; there is sign of digging around the big Korean pine trees. This is wonderful country. The big live oaks are lovely. It's good to be off alone; I find a bear-ripped honey tree and an old yurt on top of the ridge—built by an Udege trapper or maybe Chinese ginseng hunter, possibly in the time of Dersu.

Dimitri signals for me to rejoin the group. We drop back down to the Amba bottomland, finding an old trail. Suddenly,

Dimitri stops in his tracks and motions me forward. A tiger track glistens in the mud. The track in the wallow appears to be only a day or less old and more than five inches across—the print of a young but dominant male cat that leaves scrapes every hundred meters and spray scents on territorial tree markers. A poacher recently killed the previous Alpha male tiger, Dimitri says. We stop at such a tree. A bear, also attracted to the strong scent, has rubbed off the bark. I get down on my knees and press my nose against the bare trunk. I wonder who this young but freshly dominant male tiger will become? The pungent fetor of tiger fills my nostrils and—for just seconds—I travel with the big cat, orange and black stripes flashing barely perceptibly through the sea of green, undulating cone fern, into the wild and predatory world that not so very long ago was my own.

The next afternoon we board the small bus that will haul us to the railroad. The tall Udege who dumped his boat and lost his rifle shakes my hand goodbye and gives me a stick of moose jerky for the journey.

Brokaw assures Dimitri he will speak for the Bikin, for its tigers and trees. He will, Tom says, deal directly with Yeltsin's office.

The bus bounces over a rutted track out of the forest and into clear-cuts, finally dumping out on a paved road pitted with huge potholes and lined with purple iris and brown-eyed Susans. Magpies scold from the log poles that support the primitive phone line. We are stopped at a checkpoint: "Speak no English," Dimi says. The trees give way to pastureland with groves of birches and small farms that have large gardens planted against the hard winter ahead. In the gray distance, three large chimneys rise into the western horizon, the huge smokestacks of a power-generating plant, hallmarks of the industrial promise of Russia, whose failure leaves the future of this vast ancestral landscape, the greatest uncut forest on Earth, as endangered as the big cat that still prowls the Siberian taiga.

Jib and Doug inspect an old log-drop
snare near the Amba River, a branch of
the Bikin, in the Russian Far East, 1992.
RICK RIDGEWAY

Epilogues

1996

In February 1996, Dimitri and Dr. Dale Miquelle completed the most comprehensive tiger census ever, involving 665 trackers. After analysis, they conclude the Siberian tiger population contains about 350 adults and 100 subadults—good news, though the cats remain endangered by logging and poaching.

1997

A Siberian tiger attacks, kills, and eats a man named Markov four miles north of the lower Amba River in the Bikin River drainage—the same place Dimitri showed me the tracks of the young male tiger in 1992. Markov was a poacher who had previously hunted and wounded the huge cat. This payback, this vendetta, took place during December 1997. Our friend, Russian biologist Dimitri Pikunov, first chronicled the predatory tiger incident in 1998. The details of this particular tiger kill, however, constituted such a good story that they were later rewritten into a commercially successful book.

It took me another decade to splice together the personal significance of the 1997 attack. By that time, I was writing my own book, *In the Shadow of the Sabertooth*, exploring the possibility that late-Pleistocene carnivores—the huge American lion, the saber-toothed cat, and the gigantic, short-faced bear—discouraged and culled ice-age colonizers by appropriating their hunting kills and maybe eating a few two-legged pilgrims in open country.

Here's what I was thinking about: A seminal moment in the life of a hunter arrives when he finds himself the hunted. For a dreaded second, he is frozen in his tracks at the edge of the meadow by the eerie silence in the forest. He feels a primordial but familiar tenseness clamping the back of his neck and he realizes that he is being stalked as prey by a large carnivore.

This ancient relationship doesn't present itself to the modern world as frequently as it did before the industrial age or, especially, during the last days of the Pleistocene. Seeing ourselves as prey was certainly a dominant emotional reality during most of our three hundred thousand years of human evolution. But in fact, predation on human beings is so uncommon today that when a single lion, bear, or tiger emerges from the bush to stalk, kill, and sometimes eat a human it generates international news and best-selling books.

The author of *The Tiger* provides a few details of the Markov attack. In 1997, the Russian investigating officer who was tracking the tiger reported, "It looks at first like a heap of laundry until one sees the boots, luminous stubs of broken bone protruding from the tops, the tattered shirt with an arm still fitted to one of the sleeves. [He] had never seen a fellow human so thoroughly and gruesomely annihilated." The author writes, "Here, amid the twigs and leaf litter, not far from his small cabin, is all that remains of Vladimir Ilyich Markov." The tiger that killed, dismembered, and ate Markov waited for him a long time, perhaps days, lurking near the door of his cabin in the Bikin River drainage of the Russian Far East.

This huge male tiger had previously destroyed everything that had smelled of Markov, and then waited for him to come home. The attack seemed chillingly premeditated.

About this time, as I read on, a chill ran up my own neck. Something about this tiger sounded familiar. How old was this cat? I reread the book but all I could definitively find was this was a very large male tiger. I think male Siberian tigers, like grizzlies, continue to grow in size with age. Tigers can live to be fourteen years old or so in the wild, although large tigers tend to be targeted by poachers and are therefore rare. The tiger that ate Markov was later killed but never weighed. An experienced eyewitness said he had "never seen a tiger as big as that one."

Amur tiger caught by a trail camera.
Sikhote-Alin Biosphere Reserve, Russian
Far East. WCS RUSSIA

A male Siberian tiger maintains an exclusive range, driving younger males away or killing them. Russian tigers have huge territories. Could the killer tiger be ten years old? Possibly. I do the math. Probably. Dimitri Pikunov would know for sure. Is the killer tiger the same one we trailed in 1992? Yes, I think so. My instincts say it is the same mythic beast. We crossed the tracks of the tiger in question four miles southeast of the Markov attack site.

If the huge male tiger that killed, dismembered, and ate Markov in 1997 was ten years old, then it was quite likely the same cat whose scent I snorted in 1992 on the Amba River. Dimitri Pikunov would know for sure if he is still alive.

Our lives are frail, so full of wonder and beauty—the journey never ends, except as they all must.

2015

Another decade later, after many trips and a half a world away, I get an e-mail from my dear friend Rick Ridgeway, who has been sharing an adventure with Doug Tompkins, Jib Ellison, and Yvon Chouinard in Chile: "Doug and I flipped in a double kayak in cold water. Jib and others did an absolutely valiant effort to get us in. Doug died of hypothermia and I just made it—barely."

2016

Three months later, Jib, Rick, and I squat around a roaring mesquite fire deep in the desert wilderness near the Mexican border. We pour wine down our throats and spit exploding whiskey into the fire. We howl at the owls and poorwills, and laugh and weep in the flickering light. We grill our thick, bloody steaks and toast our friends, alive and departed. A meteor flashes out of Cassiopeia.

After Doug died in Chile, Yvon pulled me aside in California at Doug's memorial and told me Rick had gone over to the other side with Tompkins into death and hadn't made it all the way back yet, much the same way as I had walked as far into death with Ed Abbey as I could. It took me a long time to come back to the living.

The next morning, Jib, Rick, and I bury all traces of our camp, pack up, and drive up into the mountain range. The three of us strike out across the bajada, aim for a distant volcanic peak, and drop our packs beyond a rim of basalt. We are here for an honoring, a ceremony. This is the grave of Edward Abbey, where three friends and I buried him twenty-seven years ago. Doug Tompkins is buried in South America, but today he will be here with us. It's also the anniversary of the Mỹ Lai massacre that I unknowingly witnessed on my last day in Vietnam, flying up the South China Sea coast. A year later, the photographs in *Life* magazine changed my life.

Jib reads a poem he has written for his dearest friend. Rick and I are carrying offerings; I leave Doug a Zuni bear effigy in memory of the kayak trip the two of us took in the Queen Charlotte Islands in coastal British Columbia, looking for big bears. Rick speaks softly, telling the mountain about Doug's love of beauty.

We grieve and laugh, lingering to pour a little Mexican beer on Ed's grave for old times' sake. A pair of turkey vultures soar over, headed out to the vast bajada below.

It is our day of the dead.

Down along the border in the Arizona
desert country, Jib, Rick, and Doug
hold a wake for Doug Tompkins.
DOUG PEACOCK COLLECTION

CHEATING
ROBINSON CRUSOE

One personal circle of happiness is being deserted on a desert island. Actually, any island will do as long as it is unoccupied and I am largely abandoned to forage for myself. I figure I have contently wasted nearly half a year of my life on such islands: the wild islets of the Sea of Cortez, the islands in the High Arctic of northern Canada, or the archipelagos of coastal British Columbia.

Going alone works best. This indulgence is less the reflection of an adventurous spirit than the product of limited social ambitions. Marinating in a Montana February snowstorm, one's mood grows bilious. Island solitude can be the perfect antidote.

Of course, you can't always go solo.

Previous spread: Doug and Andrea's tent, happily situated on a deserted Belize cay, 1998. PEACOCK FAMILY COLLECTION

The place I'd picked for this outing was not in the desert seas, but off the southern coast of Belize, a country Round River Conservation Studies (I was board chair) had chosen for a jaguar project—an animal I was smitten with since my 1985 grizzly search in Mexico's Sierra Madre.

While scouting Belize's jaguar country, I noticed and visited a few islands or cays, some inhabited, others not. On the smaller islands it was still possible to get off by yourself. My role model would be Robinson Crusoe because there were old fishing camps on the islands with a lot of good junk lying around. Also, the forgiving winter weather, warm transparent Caribbean waters, great fishing, and protective barrier reefs made the dozens of cays south of Dangriga a good place to check out—to see if you could get by on your own out there without any outside support.

I loved doing this kind of thing. In the privacy of your island solitude you could indulge your deepest childhood fantasies of discovery and exploration—still this old man's credo.

I was short on the necessary cash to get down to Belize, and pitched a magazine so I could pay for the flight down and buy a saltwater reverse osmosis pump I would need for fresh water. Shamelessly, deceitfully, I mentioned Robinson Crusoe and his man Friday, knowing full well that if I left my girlfriend behind, I'd return to an empty house.

We packed everything we needed for a couple of weeks—some food, snorkeling and fishing tackle, shelter, and survival gear. The money from the magazine made it possible to buy the pump. I wanted to push the limits of this kind of "islanding" by seeing how far we could go making our own drinking water, catching fish, and living off conch and coconut.

To get around, I borrowed a sea kayak from my Montana neighbor, Tom Brokaw. We had gone on that Siberian tiger trip in the Russian Far East with mutual friends, and Tom had been kind enough to buy two Feathercraft folding kayaks and lend me his spare for the Siberian trip. I wrote Brokaw a postcard: "May I have the loan of your kayak again? In event of my non-return, I hereby assign to you as collateral my '86 Ford pickup." I have no water signs in my horoscope, and I was worried about this. The day I left for Belize, the apprehension resurfaced and I wrote Brokaw a final postcard: "The keys to the pickup are under the seat."

For my girl, Andrea, I hit up my pool-playing partner and friend, wilderness hero Mike Matz, for his Klepper, another folding kayak with a hundred-year company heritage.

And so, Andrea and I set off on our phony Robinson Crusoe adventure, aware that many a relationship has shipwrecked on the isle of isolation.

I picked a spot on the map of Belize where my departed mentor, the archaeologist Mark Papworth, once saw a jaguar track on the beach. Thus, we embarked from the Rum Point Inn, a great place to gather generous intelligence. We were looking for a small, uninhabited cay, narrow enough to walk across, mostly covered by mangroves, but with higher spots with palms where we could set up a tent. The mangroves ensure hordes of biting insects that will keep casual visitors at bay.

The next day we hired a boat and steered northeast for a low line of palm trees marking a tiny island that seemed to float on the horizon, a green apparition perched upon a featureless, lime-colored ocean. The gracious boatman, Captain Young, dropped us off with all our gear on the little cay and then turned around and headed back to the mainland.

We stood on a spit of sand. On the high end are coconut palms. Beyond, in the interior of the cay, grow mangroves. The boat disappeared into the horizon, and we surveyed our new home.

This living-off-the-land stuff isn't for everyone. That's why I try to do these trips solo—not to torture my companions. I have driven more than a few recreation-oriented chums nuts on similar trips by wasting time trying to catch dinner or dig shellfish instead of leisurely drinking a beer and chewing jerky on the beach. Now I have Andrea to feed, a caring gesture but also potentially excruciating since I don't quite know what I'm doing. Foraging off the land and sea is easiest in the Pacific Northwest. And you can dig for shellfish all around Mexico. I know nothing about these Caribbean islands beyond the magazine pictures of conchs lying all over the ocean floor and schools of colorful fish. A lot of these places have been fished out for conch, and I've never gotten around to researching the how-to-fly-fish-the-Caribbean literature. We could starve.

Losing belly fat is more likely. I had stubbornly brought only a fly rod and my own hand-tied flies to fish with, when anyone knows that a twenty-pound leader wrapped around a beer can tied to a jig gives you the best chance of snagging lunch.

My plan is to set up camp and snorkel the coral reefs to scout out where and how to catch some fish. The arrogance is unspeakable; subsistence people had generations of indigenous experience to guide them.

The view is idyllic. On the lee side of the island is a sandy flat where bonefish ghost the shallows and I see what looks like a permit fin farther out. At the moment, a stiff breeze blows from the west, precluding fly casting, but the wind also keeps the bugs at bay.

We carefully choose a tent spot among but not under the palms so ten-pound coconut cannonballs don't rain down on us during a windy night. You can see the sand flat and also the outer edge where Virginia rails scamper over mangrove roots. We gather dry driftwood for an evening fire and assemble the folding kayaks.

About a dozen islands are visible from here, though north winds make traveling to the distant ones difficult, maybe even

Kayaks borrowed from Mike Matz and
Tom Brokaw allowed Doug and Andrea
to hop among the small islands off Belize,
1998. PEACOCK FAMILY COLLECTION

risky. I carry navigational charts, and Captain Young had explained to me which cays can be camped upon, which are privately owned or otherwise occupied, and which islands get visited by dive boats or ignored. The far-flung southern cays, the Sapodilla and Silk, tend to be sandy and relatively bug-free but see a lot of kayakers and divers on the spectacular coral walls and white beaches. Other cays are private research stations or bird sanctuaries. It's not quite a wilderness but, in these days before coral bleaching, the reefs are vibrant colors and teeming with life.

We must see what's down there, as our logistical challenges focus on food and fresh water. Grabbing our snorkeling gear, I pull on my reef-walkers, slap on bug dope, and the two of us head across the tip of the narrow, quarter-mile-long island. I wade into the surf out beyond a few coral heads to waist-deep where the ocean bottom begins to fall off steeply, and I pull down my face mask. Over and in the reef hover thousands of fish—lots of them. Schools of yellowtail, snapper, barracuda, and several species of reef jack cruise by, along with angelfish, wrasse, snapper, grunt, grouper, parrot, and trumpet fish.

Despite the warm Caribbean water, I am shaking with the anticipation of hooking a big one and feeding my mate a worthy seafood dinner. Piecing together a four-piece, nine-foot, eight-weight, graphite fly rod, I select one of the gaudy flies I tied at Jeff Bridges's house during the brutal Montana winter of 1996–97, a deceiver pattern. I pinch a split-shot on the leader and cast beyond the blue line marking the drop-off. Giving the big fly a moment to sink, I strip in as fast as I can. I try again and again. I slow down the retrieve. Nothing. My stomach growls. I wish I'd read the saltwater fishing book. Getting these suckers to bite the fly is harder than it looked when swimming among them. For a moment I have an unethical desire for a stick of dynamite.

The sun is beginning to drop down to the horizon, a fiery red globe beyond thin clouds—a brief transition from daylight to darkness in the tropics and the best time for getting a thousand bites from the no-see-ums boiling out of the mangroves. More bug dope. We return to camp, fishless, and light a fire. We need more water for the night, so I grab the freshwater pump.

Wading into the lee of the tiny island, I fill a waterproof bag—it keeps the sand out of the filter—with saltwater. I take out the twenty-two-inch-long pump and lay it across my lap. I sit under a listing palm and look out on a broad flat while I work. Submerging the intake strainer in the river-bag, I begin to pump the handle of the reverse osmosis pump, an arduous process that supposedly produces a quart of drinking water in about ten minutes, depending on your waning energies. This is a lot harder than the brochure made out; making two weeks of fresh water could turn you into a one-armed Arnold Schwarzenegger.

Brown pelicans dive-bomb baitfish a hundred feet south of the red mangroves. An osprey screams, circling overhead. The wind abates and shifts; I can smell the tannic pungency of leaves rotting along the shoreline. Ten minutes later, I spot a bonefish tailing on the edge of the flat. Farther out, a dark fin slices the skin of the ocean, emerges then disappears—probably an eagle ray or small nurse shark.

Within thirty minutes my arm is tired, but I have enough water to see us through the night. I'm hungry as hell and, sheepishly, I think about disappointing my patient mate. I needed to catch something to eat. We carry rice, tabouli, tsampa, oat cereal, chiltepin, and condiments, but no real food. Each day, I must catch fish or find shellfish to avoid the monotony of our veggie diet. I like to put a little pressure on myself when I go out like this. My girl Friday, however, may have a different agenda.

Back at camp, I rekindle twigs with dry palm bark and coconut husks. I add driftwood until I have a small fire blazing at the

Palms shadow the bonefish flats. You
don't want to pitch your tent under a
coconut tree where a strong wind could
pitch a cannonball-sized nut on your head.
PEACOCK FAMILY COLLECTION

beach just above the high-tide mark. A few mosquitoes and no-see-ums are out, but the night breeze keeps them down. After we gum down tin plates of gruel, I reach into the bow of my kayak, hoping to partially compensate for my failure as a fisherman, and pull out a luxury—a single bottle of local booze. I mix two fat fingers of Belize rum with lime juice (a poor man's gimlet, not half bad) in my canteen cup, lie back, and snuggle with Andrea, sharing the appeasement.

We awake to an immaculate sky, restless to explore. About a dozen islands are clearly visible in the morning haze. The sea is calm and if it stays that way, we could reach any one of them in the kayak by noon. One of the closest islands is decorated with big palms; the other cays are mostly mangroves, sometimes known as wet cays. These places provide great habitat for birds and, especially, bugs. For this reason, they are seldom visited by kayakers or tourists. The fishing and diving are also great around these islands, where there is seldom enough dry land to pitch a tent. Most of these small islands are formed when red mangrove seeds pioneer shifting sandbars. These seedlings can survive afloat for a year at sea and may come from thousands of miles away. Once fortified in the shoals, they anchor the sand, and in time, mangroves and palms grow, providing habitat for countless marine creatures and nesting birds.

I start a fire and heat water for coffee, then wade out into the sand flat and take a wake-up bath, already tingling with anticipation. For me, the chance to camp with Andrea on a deserted island is a dream. There's scarcely enough time in the Caribbean day to explore the islands, see the birds, dive the coral forests, fish the flats and drop-offs for food, and consider kayaking out to the neighboring islands.

I lean back against the trunk of a palm tree with my feet on the sandy beach, pumping the day's water. A mild breeze rustles the sawgrass and runs over the shoals. I work the pump and make three quarts of water, remembering places and imagining the islands I could explore using the pump and the fold-up kayak and camping gear: coastal Alaska and British Columbia, desert islands off Baja, or the dry archipelagos of New Guinea and Indonesia. You could go almost anywhere fishable waters are navigable by kayak and get by—or not—on your own skills and wits.

Here on our "uninhabitable" island, we are as happy as pigs in swill. We glass the two closest islands to the west: one is low and gray, a wet cay; the other, smaller island sprouts a sizable grove of palm trees. We'll go check out both of them by kayak as soon as the winds are suitable. Beauty is everywhere.

About midday, we decide to cautiously paddle into the wind, thinking if we get into trouble the waves would bring us back to camp. A stiff northerly breeze races over the Belize Barrier Reef. I aim the sixteen-foot sea kayak against the wind and paddle hard into three-foot waves that occasionally wash over the bow. Off to my left, dark clouds hang on the distant mainland coastline. That makes me nervous. Though I'm not quite a novice at open-water sea kayaking, I'm close enough to watch my step here. Andrea's athleticism makes her a natural. The weather has been unsettled for days and it looks like we're not going to make the reef today—too much wind and too much open ocean for a safe trip.

We spin the sea kayaks 180 degrees, then paddle hard for the tiny cay. We need to get back to our camp before dark. The surging wind-driven waves on our stern drive us to the shore of the little island a couple of hours before sunset. We steer around coral heads and land our crafts on a sandy beach below an overhanging palm tree.

I try fishing for dinner, despite my prior record of botched casting to limitless schools of fish. Skipping a duct-tape squid fly over coral heads and retrieving, again I fish poorly. My hopes sink with the sun. Then, miraculously, I am finally hit on the retrieve by a small but strong fish. I don't want to lose this one. I play the fish around the fan coral and walk the foot-long yellowtail snapper up to the beach. Dinner.

We sit on the beach enjoying the sunset, then return to camp and watch the fire.

When it has burned down a bit, I rake out a pile of coals and place the fish, wrapped in aluminum foil with a tad of soy and dill in the cavity, on the embers and then pile more coals on top. Overhead, we can make out Gemini through a hole in the clouds. In ten minutes, the fish is ready; supper is brown rice, hot sauce, lime, and hour-fresh fish.

Using a flashlight, I store the leftovers where the hermit crabs won't run off with them, strip off my clothes, and crawl into the tent with Andrea. A gentle breeze rustles in the palms and saw-grass. A tiny gust wafts through the mosquito netting by my head and I remember a hundred nights spent sleeping in this tent. I pull out a paperback of Hemingway stories and read for a few minutes before I realize how tired I am.

During the night, the tent is buffeted by winds and pelted by a half-hour tropical rainstorm. At least three heavy coconuts thud down nearby. I snuggle against Andrea's warmth.

We awake to great-tailed grackles squabbling over nesting territory. Brown pelicans dive on small fish driven by larger nee-dlefish along the mangroves. By the time I drag myself out of the tent, the sky has cleared. Scudding clouds hang on the coast of Belize far to my northwest. I take out my binoculars to check out birds moving in the mangrove roots and singing overhead: Virginia rail, ruddy turnstone, tiger heron, mangrove warbler, and royal tern.

We move the tent, looking for the most scenic campsite— there are many. The morning is warm, and I snorkel off the south side of the island. The sandy beach falls off into lovely coral

Andrea cleans shellfish for dinner, 1998.
Belize. PEACOCK FAMILY COLLECTION

gardens where thousands of reef fish cruise the colorful habitat. I spot the pointed ends of pen shells sticking out of the ocean floor, dive down, and pull up several for dinner. The hinge muscle of the pen shell, however, is small, and what I'd really like is a big conch. So far only Andrea has scored: a single small conch and a big turban snail. Where are all those gigantic shellfish you see lying around in all the diving magazines? There's a pile of big, harvested conch shells on the beach telling that story. I did see a pair of antennae, I presumed belonging to a spiny lobster, sticking out from under a huge rock—impossible to retrieve. This easy living in the cays is tougher than I thought it would be. This little trip is looking to be the equivalent of three weeks at the Fat Farm.

A mixed flock of pelicans, boobies, gulls, and terns have been diving on a giant school of baitfish and the feeding frenzy seems to be moving my way. I rig up a wire tippet on the end of a fifteen-pound leader and tie on a huge gaudy fly that looks like a small parrot with a bad haircut. I tuck the fly rod under the elastic cord on the bow of the kayak and push off, aiming downwind directly in the path of the approaching diving birds. What kinds of fish are under there herding up the baitfish? The wind is driving the kayak and I'll only have time for a couple of casts.

The ocean boils and churns with escaping anchovies and diving birds. A couple of mackerel-like fins slice the surface and below there are flashes of bigger fish. I cast in front of the seething waters, something strikes, and I miss. I cast back again and am hit by what looks like a baby tuna; nuts, time is limited, and I wanted a bigger one. I horse the ten-inch fish in and drop it at my feet in the cockpit of the kayak.

Turning the kayak upwind, I paddle fiercely for two minutes and catch up with the feeding fish. This time I punch the fly into the center of the ball of baitfish. I strip the line in and am immediately hit by a big fish that makes a run. The reel screams, then I haul back on the rod and try to turn the fish. Somehow I manage, awkwardly maneuvering the kayak with one hand on the paddle.

In five minutes, I bring the forty-inch barracuda alongside the kayak. There is no way I can land the fish or drag it through the fan coral to shore. You don't want to share a kayak cockpit with a critter capable of taking off half your leg. I reach down with a gloved hand and needle-nosed pliers to carefully grab the hook that is inches from rows of sharp teeth. A quick twist and lift on the hook releases the aggressive fish; it drifts away and then turns and swims into the blue. I've got to figure out a way to land these fish; they're usually easy to hook and I'm unusually hungry.

Later in the morning, I scrounge an old conch camp on the island looking for scraps of metal to construct a lobster spear, gaff, or net for landing barracuda. The pieces of nylon net caught up in mangrove roots have rotted in the sun and I give up on the net idea. Several nails, however, protrude from the trunk of a palm tree. I manage to extract one #16 common and two small finishing nails. The rest of the morning is spent hammering and using the file on my knife to sharpen the big nail and file two broad sloping notches on either side, where I'll anchor the finishing nails as barbs. But two nails are too much work and I settle for a single barb. I learn slowly by trial and error—mostly error.

The filing and shaping takes up the bulk of the day. My mind wanders and I remember carrying an eight-foot spear on another island, in another country. I snap out of the reverie and finish the filing. Securing the haft is the next problem and I comb the old camp for another hour before finding a treasure hoard of baling wire, four or five feet in all, mostly rusted, but with short sections of uncorroded metal.

The rest of the spear-making goes fast: I wrap the wire around the head of the small nail, anchoring it in one of the two notches, then touch up the tip of the spear with a small

Doug fishes poorly; skunked again
on a Belize bonefish flat, 1998.
PEACOCK FAMILY COLLECTION

whetstone. A four-foot section of broomstick-like driftwood will be the shaft. I carve a groove for the big nail, with a slit at the end for the head, and lash the whole thing with nylon cord. The spearhead is just long enough to handle a big lobster or a medium barracuda.

Twilight gathers under the palms. I grab my fly rod and walk into the surf, continuing east into the coral heads, then wading south down the island paralleling the shoreline until I am opposite the mangroves. Fish are feeding along the stilt-like roots: big fish. I cast a tarpon fly into the trees and strip in the line as rapidly. On the second jerk, the water explodes. I haul back and set the hook, feeling the weight of a huge fish. A long dorsal fin dances violently and briefly on the dark water. The line goes slack and a wake of water from the escaping fish washes the shoreline. Rats, a fish that big would have kept us in food for two or three days.

I reel in and examine the leader: it is cleanly clipped off, with rows of teeth marking another four inches of monofilament. A big barracuda? In the dying light, I struggle to tie on a steel-wire tippet and attach another fly. I breathe heavily, smelling the fetor of mangrove leaves rising on the evening humidity. My heart slows a bit and I cast again into the mangroves. I am hit immediately by another cuda, a smaller one that I play up into the shallows and impale with the lobster spear.

Illuminated by a popping fire of dry driftwood, I fillet the barracuda, then cube the flesh. I take my time, savoring every minute of cooking, every morsel of food. We make a rum drink out of dried fruit and coconut milk. The small tuna is filleted, cut into sashimi strips, which we inhale raw as an appetizer with tamari sauce and wasabi mixed from powder. We add the cubes of cut barracuda to lime juice, diced onion and garlic, and tomato from a small salsa can. I clean the pen shells and remove and dice the meat of the raw conch. The oily barracuda and cubes of shellfish will cure from the acidity of lime and tomato during the night, rendering the lot into a fine ceviche.

The next day, we push off for the nearest mangrove island, Tarpon Cay. The tailwind is brisk and we arrive at the north end of the cay in good time to tie up the kayaks and suit up for a dive. The bottom drops off rapidly to a bench, ten to twenty feet deep, compartmentalized into lovely gardens by huge columns of coral. The reef fish are more abundant here than anywhere I've seen in Belize. I glide through the fan corals to the drop-off where a school of five big bonito cruise by. The coral and the reef fish are pristine.

We continue exploring the rest of the island with snorkel and mask. Hundreds of egrets, both cattle and common, roost in the mangroves. Brown pelicans and boobies dive on the half-beak fish that scoot along the surface fleeing larger fish. The island is less than a half mile long and shaped like a fishhook with the bend opening to the southwest. I swim south into the hook. Birds are everywhere, green and tiger herons, grackles, and warblers. I turn into a big hole. The water is murky here. The water boils with small fish. I can see big silver flashes deeper in the hole.

Underwater visibility is limited. Something is biting or stinging me, maybe isopods or jellyfish. I'd been told there used to be saltwater crocodiles here. I tense and glimpse something big and shiny in the hole. Probably tarpon, but a reptilian premonition creeps up my spine and I quickly lose my curiosity. I turn back. The sun is setting, the wind howling, and it's time to get back to camp.

As the sun drops into the Maya Mountains fifty miles to the west, we turn our kayaks into the wind and paddle hard, putting all our strength into getting to our island before dark. Though I carry a compass and flashlight around my neck, it would be easy to miss one of these little islands in the dark—potentially dangerous, though we could probably make it back to the insect-infested mangroves for a miserable night if we had to. We paddle steadily for another half hour. The gray mass of the island hangs in the gloom of evening. We paddle on, digging deep, two engines heading into the darkness. Andrea says she can't keep up. We can't separate in the gloom; we could die out here in the darkness of the open ocean.

I take Andrea's bow line and tie it to my stern. Together, we paddle into the wind. I think I can make out a fading grayness on the horizon. We pull with all our strength toward the spot where we guess the island is. Just as darkness falls, I catch the outline of a palm tree. We made it. Exhausted but safe, we land, kindle a fire, and warm our toes.

On Wednesday morning, our seventh day (I checked my notebook), we pack up all our gear and move it to the head of the island, next to the big sand flat. Captain Young will pick us up tomorrow. I want one more day of getting skunked fishing on the bonefish flat. So far, the stiff wind in my face has precluded graceful casting. In fact, the only bonefish I've ever caught have been by accident. I have two friends who are world-class bonefish champions, Carl Hiaasen and Yvon Chouinard. I wish they were here to guide me. Most every time I toss a fly toward the cruising fish, they scatter like pigs before the gun.

I wade out around a few fan corals decorating the sandy flat. Andrea sits on the beach watching. The west wind is rising, blowing in my face. I can see fish shadows moving on the bottom of the flat: bonefish. Farther out, I see a tail and a dorsal fin breaking the surface, no doubt a fabled permit or pompano, both hard-fighting jackfish. My gear is a little light for permit, but if I can make a sufficiently long cast, maybe I could land a little one; they are the best eating. I stalk along the sandbar and

An evening dip on the flats, 1998. Belize.
PEACOCK FAMILY COLLECTION

make a long cast, trying for the permit. My fly splashes on the water. The permit startles in a cloud of sand and races off the flat. Trounced again.

The wind gusts and salt spray peppers my face and forearms. I join Andrea on the beach and give myself over to the sensual pleasures of this beautiful place, enjoying the vault of high cirrus in an otherwise immaculate blue sky, pelicans off the point, frigatebirds circling overhead.

The next morning, I scramble up the beach and grab my binoculars; a boat is headed in our direction and it is the Rum Point dive boat. I hold Andrea's hand and we watch Captain Young as he eases the jet boat through the coral heads, into the shallows, and reverses the engine.

GALÁPAGOS

Rick Bass and Terry Tempest Williams pinned me to a giant rock in the middle of Montana's Centennial Valley and extracted a promise that I'd meet up with them in South America on the fifteenth anniversary of Ed Abbey's death. The rock I was pinned against was smooth in places because, Rick and Terry told me, ancient bison rubbed against it through time immemorial. I was skeptical, as it had been a long time since any bison had ranged here and there were cows all over the place. Still, these two close friends had taught me much over the decades and I had to listen. They were among the wisest colleagues I had trekked with. Terry was an expert birder; just the night before, she had pointed out Virginia rails scooting in the high grass and sedge on the shore of Red Rock Lake. You couldn't see them, just the grass moving, the rails revealed by their *tick-it* calls.

The place they made me agree to meet them was the Galápagos down in Ecuador, a group of islands famous for their birds, among other things. Though I come from a family skilled in bird identification, I was a third-rate birder, always wondering if I had correctly seen the diagnostic bars or crests or stripes on the

Previous spread: Spine of a Galápagos marine iguana. LAUREL PEACOCK

Above: Rick Bass, Terry Tempest Williams, and Doug (left to right) in the Galápagos, 2014. You can learn things from these people, Doug's dearest pals. LAUREL PEACOCK

Andrea Peacock aboard the *Samba* on the
equatorial waters of the Galápagos, 2014.
LAUREL PEACOCK

departing wings. I'd have to cram on the feathered ones over the winter so I didn't make a fool of myself in front of my accomplished friends.

On March 14, 2014, we cross the equator by boat off the northwest tip of Isabela Island: the Ecuadorian Galápagos. A couple of bottlenose dolphins race the bow of our ship, and the ocean below shimmers with perceptible energy as if a giant leviathan hovers just below the surface.

Boobies, pelicans, and hundreds of a species of petrels I have never seen before dive-bomb the anchovies we see leaping free of the rippling sea, escaping the bonito and albacore tuna below them. Phalaropes float on mats of insects. Noddies follow the brown pelicans, and magnificent frigatebirds soar above, swooping down to steal baitfish from the diving birds. A surge of gulls and storm petrels breaks in front of the boat, following the anchovies, rolling from one patch of frothing ocean to another; bloody chunks of baitfish litter the surface. Far ahead, I can see the giant fins of sunfish breaking the waves. A number of my boatmates jump off to swim across the invisible equatorial line. They say the water is freezing.

We are riding on a seventy-eight-foot, steel-hulled, refitted fishing boat named the *Samba*. This ship is plush with hot water and air conditioning. On board are a crew of seven, a naturalist, and thirteen fellow travelers, half of whom I have never met before. When we land to visit the wildlife, we're not supposed to touch anything. It is exactly the kind of cruise I have carefully avoided for the past four decades.

Nonetheless, as an old soldier with a foot in the grave, I'm working on my bucket list (trips to the Arctic and Africa are also on it) and this cushy, seemingly indulgent journey to these well-tended islands—planned with two close friends and two family members—is number one. Rick and Terry are aboard, along with Andrea and Laurel Peacock, my wife and daughter.

For more than four decades, I have done my best to protect wild places, grizzly bears, and other top predators. After this trip, I will head to the North Slope of the Yukon, where polar bears are interbreeding with grizzlies. The summer sea ice in the Arctic's Beaufort Sea will soon be completely gone and the permafrost is already heaving, beginning to release heavy gasps of methane into the atmosphere. It looks like a worldwide warming of 5 degrees Fahrenheit and up to a dozen feet of sea rise could arrive sooner than the end of the century, as the mainstream press has dangerously underestimated. The rate of climate change is mind-boggling. I am seeking clarity in this madness. Humans have glimpsed the mirror that reflects their own extinction. The isolated Galápagos, as yet only slightly touched by climate change, seem something sane I can wrap my mind around.

After a sleepless night motoring over pitching seas, we aim for Darwin Bay, a volcanic caldera cookie-cut into the edge of Genovesa Island, though Charles Darwin never ventured there. The best thing about the northern and western Galápagos is that the smaller islands, including this one, are uninhabited by humans. The *Samba's* Zodiacs unload us on a flat beach swarming with red-footed boobies. Male frigatebirds puff out their red throats trying to attract females, swallow-tailed gulls regurgitate squid pieces for their chicks, and mated boobies preen each other, pausing to upchuck a half-digested fish for the kids. A sea lion pup plays in a tide pool. Everywhere reeks of the smells and sounds of reproduction, and the cries and squawks of birds mingle in raucous chorus.

We get to snorkel Darwin Bay. Sea lions loop around us. There are balls of wrasses, schools of angelfish, snappers, parrotfish, and grunts—dozens more species that I cannot name and more fish than anyone could ever count. My daughter, Laurel, grabs me and points to a sizable, fleeing hammerhead shark.

A male magnificent frigatebird, *Fregata magnificens*, puffs out his inflatable red pouch during the breeding season. Galápagos. LAUREL PEACOCK

Winging their way over the ocean bottom are dozens of golden cownose rays. These schools, flocks, herds, swarms of life—fish, birds, mammals, or insects, it doesn't seem to matter what the species or size is—satisfy an ancient human need to experience animals in multitude, like watching a herd of a million bison or a flock of passenger pigeons that blacked out the sun for three days while it passed. I wouldn't care to live in a world without such a possibility.

Back on Genovesa, we climb up steps carved out of the basalt to a mesa-like plateau ruled by Nazca boobies. Frigatebirds roost in the arid, deciduous low trees. Short-eared owls squat in shallow lava tubes. Down on the shoreline, we see turnstones rolling big pumice rocks and whimbrels amid a shifting tide of plovers dodging the breaking surf. Flocks of red-billed tropicbirds squawk but soar gracefully above. These tern-like flyers nest in the cliffs and make clumsy landings, encumbered by their graceful tail that can grow twice as long as their body. A testosterone-fueled Nazca booby blocks the return trail and snaps at each of us as we pass.

Our boat guide, Juan, discourses at length on the testosterone levels in Nazca boobies, bird mating patterns, and the reproductive advantages of aggression and social monogamy. My wife, Andrea, whispers, "Maybe it's been a long time since he had a girlfriend." Our two local guides are well read, biologically literate, and, best of all, versed in solid evolutionary theory (recent Galápagos fundamentalist churches have produced a plague of creationist guides). But even the best of guides are reluctant to go too far to paint a less-than-rosy picture of a human history where land tortoises have been slaughtered into extinction, and Galápagos hawks, historically the islands' top predator, pushed to dangerously low numbers.

Juan tells me there are no Galápagos hawks on Genovesa because the island is too young to produce land reptiles, the lizards the hawk likes to feed on. The next day, I see a Galápagos hawk off Marchena Island. We are watching a lava lizard, as black and crenulated as the basalt it lies upon; it turns to look up at us. As if on cue, a brown raptor curls overhead. Like the Harris's hawks of my own low-desert country, these social birds hunt in groups of two or three and feed together in larger numbers. They sometimes roost on the ground, though the ones we saw were on high tree branches. With human tolerance, the hawk could probably live in nearly any Galápagos habitat, feeding on insects, lizards, smaller iguanas, rats, carrion, and sea and land birds. It has no fear of people: Charles Darwin once wrote he "... pushed [one] off a branch with the end of my gun, a large hawk."

Buteo galapagoensis, the scientific name for the Galápagos hawk, was once common on most of the main islands of the Galápagos, but suffered a serious population decline with the influx of immigrants from the mainland. It is now extinct on five islands, and the adult population is about three hundred birds. Chicken-ranching immigrants to the island perceived the hawk as a threat to their chicks and, by some accounts, solved the problem by eliminating the "tame" Galápagos hawk. More recently, the birds have been forced to compete for food with introduced feral cats.

The guides use the phrase "ecological naïveté" to explain the apparent tameness of hawks, tortoises, and other Galápagos creatures. My friend David Quammen coined that particular expression in his 1997 classic book on island biogeography, *The Song of the Dodo*. Quammen used ecological naïveté to distinguish the behavior of isolated island wildlife from tameness, the distinction being that Galápagos hawks or tortoises evolved in habitats without threats. The corollary is that the evolutionary loss of defensive behaviors, or failure to acquire new ones, in these ecologically naïve animals may render them vulnerable to new or introduced predators like mongooses, tree snakes, or

A Galápagos hawk, *Buteo galapagoensis*,
checks out a young giant tortoise on
Isabela Island, Galápagos. TUI DE ROY/
MINDEN PICTURES

feral cats. Evolution prepared the Galápagos creatures for a simpler, more innocent world.

Homo sapiens, meanwhile, evolved to deal with saber-toothed cats in the bush, bears of the night, or, especially, other humans. But a new danger has arrived, a relatively fresh enemy: The beast of today is climate change. How do we respond to a dimly perceived but deadly worldwide threat that will require a collective human resolve to mitigate? Did evolution not provide us with the wit to face the rising oceans, the melting ice, the warming Earth, and raging fires that will precariously shrink the habitats seven and a half billion people depend on? For us, ecological naïveté is not a survivable choice.

These troubling thoughts ebb as we take a swim in a warm lagoon, alive with fur seals, swarms of wrasse, and schools of larger fish indistinct against a muddy bottom. Andrea briskly swims over to Laurel and me; she pushes up her mask. She has found a colorful castle of coral, spiral corals surrounded by blue-phase sergeant majors busy snacking off the green algae growing like lawn around the castle. My bucket list again: For the past several years we have unsuccessfully searched for unbleached coral off Costa Rica, Hawai'i, and the Florida Keys. The castle is her gift to me.

The Galápagos were discovered by accident in 1535 by a Spanish cleric from Panama who found himself becalmed in the doldrums of these equatorial waters and drifted into the islands. My visit to the Galápagos constitutes, in part, an attempt to escape my own doldrums: I touch my collarbone and feel the top of a long vertical scar covering my steel-wired sternum.

The *Samba* swings around the western nose of seahorse-shaped Isabela Island and into a broad cove east of Punta Vicente Roca. We pull on wetsuits and slip into the water. Juan says, "Find your own turtle." The waves rock us back and forth against a sheer cliff where a penguin perches. Galápagos green sea turtles are everywhere, big and little ones. Something leans against my flipper and I lurch sideways to let a three hundred-pound turtle pass. Suddenly, I find myself within a squadron of swimming turtles. I spot my daughter, Laurel, noticeable with only one flipper due to her injured knee. Next to her swims my best friend, Terry Tempest Williams, also conspicuous in her rainbow wetsuit. They grab my hands and we join the broad flotilla of swimming turtles.

Riding back in the Zodiac, two of the people I most respect in the world are privately weeping. I feel a knot loosen in my chest, a shared magic with these women who make my life.

The enigmatic face of a Galápagos iguana.
LAUREL PEACOCK

REBURYING THE
ARROWHEADS

I push the aluminum canoe off the muddy bank into a side channel of the braided river. Sliding into the stern, I aim the dented craft toward the middle of the shallow canal. There is no whitewater in the Shiawassee River. Instead, it fans out onto a broad plain of cattails, punctuated here and there by low, brushy islands fringed by hardwood trees. The gradient of this river is zilch. For more than a half century, I have known this swampy region simply as the Flats.

My cousin Marc is in the bow with a blue bandana tied over his balding head. The morning sun is already up, and we look forward to a warm spring afternoon. Already, we can hear the background drone of insects and birds, highlighted by the

Previous spread: The Shiawassee National
Wildlife Refuge, also known as "the Flats,"
Saginaw County, Michigan. DAVID STIMAC

honking of geese, the quacking of mallards, and the coarse buzzing of dragonflies.

On the bottom of the canoe lie a spare paddle, a water jug, and a cooler full of cheap Michigan beer. There are other items packed in a waterproof bag—some food, clothing, and first aid items. A heavy, oiled canvas bag sits beside it. The lumpy contents are what have brought us here.

Inside the canvas bag are treasures of a lost world: arrowheads of all sizes, colors, and shapes. There are prehistoric grooved stone axes; adzes; pendants; celts; hammerstones; shaft-straighteners; flint knives; chalcedony cutting stones; six-inch-long spearheads, one with a turkey-tail base below the opposing notches; a variety of scrapers and skinning blades; and a short string of copper beads, oxidized over four thousand years into brilliant green.

These ancient goods represent the bounty of an unstructured boyhood spent combing the pastures, ridges, and swamps for the imperishable leavings of long-vanished people. Most of the objects are arrowheads, though from age eight on I picked up most any odd item I didn't recognize. Now, fifty-some years later, I want to put them all back where I found them, in the same places where discovery first shimmered off the mud of spring-plowed fields.

Repatriating the artifacts was proving to be a tough job because some of the places I looked for and found arrowheads fifty years ago are now developed: fancy houses had been built on the lonely sand ridges, and rows of townhouses had been plunked down in the cornfields of my youth. I found myself low-crawling through the gardens and hedgerows of strangers, dressed in camouflage and carrying a garden trowel with which I would insert the artifact back into the dirt in the closest place possible to where I had originally found it. This was dangerous: a scruffy outsider sneaking through suburban shrubbery could get arrested or shot.

But most of the objects in the canvas bag came from remote swamps, woodlands, and distant fields, places that look the same today as when I found them as a boy. These arrowheads are proving fun to rebury. After all, this region was my original taste of wilderness, an aboriginal quality I had sought out all my life. The Flats were the wild heart of an early homeland, where my dad had taken me for canoe trips as a nine-year-old. Now we were paddling back into them: the cattail swamps where legions of Canada geese and whistling swans had darkened the evening skies of my youth—the downy wildebeests of my watery Serengeti.

———

The Shiawassee Flats today are in a national wildlife refuge. Established in 1953, the refuge was created mostly to protect migratory birds. It's only ninety-eight hundred acres of marsh, not much on a scale with the parks and wilderness areas of our Western states, but considerable in this populated area of rural central Michigan where it's difficult to walk a linear mile without crossing a road.

Marc had once worked for the Shiawassee National Wildlife Refuge as a ranger and interpretive guide. His ranger duties might have been routine, but his naturalist skills shone when leading groups of kids on nature walks. A couple of years ago, I visited Marc at the Shiawassee Refuge's Green Point Environmental Learning Center and tagged along on one of those trips with a dozen middle-school students, learning about bugs, birds, tracks, trees, and the Native Americans who lived in these parts—and how everything hooked together. Marc's teaching deftness—honed by years in theater, polished by his poetry and slamming those poems before audiences—blew me away. The children were spellbound.

I was also hit by the fact that Marc and the kids were standing on the largest tract of uninhabited, undeveloped ground in

A cache of roughed-out prehistoric chert
blades similar to one found by Doug.
PEACOCK FAMILY COLLECTION

Saginaw County—the Flats—and yet, in prehistoric times, more people lived here than anywhere else around. The very soil upon which we stood had a rock-hard layer of dirt a few feet down that had been compacted by the tramping of human feet four thousand years ago. Green Point was a prominent village site. The ancient people who fished and hunted here were known by their distinctive arrowheads, and thousands of these artifacts had been collected here. Thousands more were still right here, and we were walking on them.

Of course, this was several years ago and Marc was a quarter century younger than me. He didn't think you could find many arrowheads just lying around anymore. I told him we needed to go for a walk.

We hiked down an old farm road, past fallow fields into a nearby woodlot that separated the agricultural land from the Shiawassee. Here along the bank, the river had eroded into the undisturbed soil and was depositing it as a narrow beach along the low water level brought on by the current drought.

I stepped over the low bank onto the beach and froze, signaling Marc to join me; next to my boot, a profusion of fire-broken rocks and chert flakes were scattered across the mud along with several freshwater mussel shells; a foot away was a big, perfect, corner-notched, chocolate-brown arrowhead.

We found fourteen more arrowheads that morning, including another smaller but perfectly matched version of the corner-notched one. These two nearly identical brown-chert arrowheads were probably part of a larger cache of such finished artifacts, buried by Native Americans about four thousand years ago as offerings—maybe to be retrieved by later people. Over the years, I had found about a dozen of these points here and most of them ended up in that oiled canvas bag in the bottom of the canoe. That day, we reburied all those arrowheads exactly where we found them.

———

Now, three years later, we paddle the canoe down a narrow passage of river lined by cattails. We are headed to more open water that spreads over the rippled flats. The sun is high on my shoulder. I guide the craft into a major channel that runs along a forest and soon braids into multiple watercourses that thread through the bulrushes. The river is only a few feet deep in this waterway and schools of carp explode in the shallows. We get out and head into the trees. Beyond is a human-made dike designed to channel the runoff so the cornfields drain. We climb up the eighty-year-old embankment, now covered with brush and poison ivy. A hen pheasant flushes. On the top of the dike are big pieces of ancient pottery, which are much younger than our corner-notched arrowheads. I explain this to Marc, though I don't understand why the potsherds are here. Are they dredged from different depths? Marc and I, dressed in earth colors to match the dirt and undergrowth, push on through to the other side of the dike. A band of shrub-like trees lies in front of us, the muted grays of early spring giving way to flowering dogwood. Beyond are fields, plowed but not planted. A mile or so to the north, we see a barn and a couple of houses.

I low-crawl through the hedgerow to the edge of the fields. Marc follows dutifully, knowing and indulging my famous paranoia, perhaps born in Vietnam. But even before the war, I had always snuck around in the woods, camouflaged, keeping to the tree line out of some ancient, maybe genetic impulse. Sharing my bloodlines, Marc accepts this aberrant behavior. I don't want anyone or anything messing with our mission.

We creep through the last bushes and emerge on the edge of a field. I resist the temptation to walk out a few hundred feet and look for arrow points. In the 1950s, I had probably picked up a hundred artifacts, mostly arrowheads, plus large canine teeth from prehistoric domestic dogs or wolves, in this

same field. Lying down in the grass, looking out over the cornfield, I slip a gallon-sized plastic bag out of the canvas bag. The
various ziplock bags contain items specific to particular sites.
Inside this plastic bag are the ancient tools that I need to rebury
somewhere around here. I think maybe we should dig a deep
hole out in the plowed field ... but, no, the stuff would just get
plowed up again.

At the edge of the field, in undisturbed soil, I dig a narrow pit
in the ground. We take turns placing the projectile points in the
hole alongside the stone axes. The last artifact to be repatriated
is a small sandstone slab with a deep groove across it. The work
goes quickly. We fill the hole and put the sod back in place.

This variety of outlaw repatriation is a lot of work and I
ask myself, why take the trouble? It's difficult and a bit dangerous—I'm too old for this. Why not simply give the artifacts
to the Tribes or a museum? Or an archaeologist? Even when I
was young, I questioned conventional archaeology: Is the highest
value these relics can have as objects of scientific scrutiny or as
the stuff of wonder and reflection for other humans to consider
their place in the world? Combing the fields and blowouts for
arrowheads in my backyard wilderness at age fourteen certainly
nudged me to think outside my time and beyond my culture.

Deep down I know the artifacts belong back out here, not
in the musty drawers of some museum. Maybe somebody else
would find them, probably not, but the fertile seed for that potential childhood leap of mind would still be there.

It was the way I grew up—awkward and alone, but adventurous—following the banks and terraces of rivers down into the
swamps, prowling the wetlands and woodlots, fishing, hunting
pheasants, and looking for old Native American camps. The con-
tours of those fens and snaking ridges created a map of my first
world, a home where discovery and exploration were always
possible. Gradually, this boyhood vision of adventure edged

into the larger world and I craved wildness beyond the wood-lots and fallow fields; it launched a lifetime aimed at boundless horizons and decades spent chasing grizzlies, tigers, jaguars, and polar bears all over the Northern Hemisphere. The value of that wandering life emerged from a kid looking for arrowheads, and then thinking about the vanished people who had made them. Where'd they come from and how did they live?

Every single relict carried its own history and a tale attached to finding it and I knew those stories by heart. I remember how I would leave middle school in early spring and head out to greet the first snow-free plowed field, the bursting emotion, the sharp anticipation of the fetor of freshly turned dirt with a flash of flaked flint gleaming in it. It was an ache to equal my surging ad-olescent hormones. Those pieces emitted mystery and a lost way of life. They spoke of another world, an older, more compelling existence that I wanted somehow to become a part of.

We go back to the canoe. It's heating up. Is it too early for a beer? The paddling is easy. We can see no other humans, al-though a jet contrail spreads across the sky. About a half-dozen miles downstream, the Shiawassee River joins the Tittabawassee to form the Saginaw River. There, the refuge ends and the city begins. Yet, the Flats feel bigger than that.

The birds are without number: Canada geese and the whis-tling swans (as my dad and I used to call them, though today they are known as tundra swans), great egrets and herons, squadrons of ducks, mergansers, scaup, teal, grebes, cormorants, harriers that we used to call marsh hawks soaring over the bulrushes, sandhill cranes, and bald eagles. For Marc and me, and for our own different reasons, the great blue heron is our favorite bird. Gulls cry and shorebirds peep. There're more sandpipers and plovers than we knew existed, yellowlegs, dunlins, and godwits. A warbler with some yellow on it flushes from a tree; neither of us know what the hell the bird is called.

The Shiawassee is awash in tracks of what
went before. Michigan. DAVID STIMAC

We drift on down the sunny river. In an eddy near the bank, a beaver smacks the water with his tail. Mussel shells bang against the bottom of the aluminum craft. The Native Americans used to feast on them, and I wonder if the shellfish are OK to eat these days. Probably not, as most midwestern rivers have been used as industrial sewers for a century. It's too shallow to float the canoe, so we get out and drag it over the shoal, driving screaming killdeer down the sandbar. The water is still cold from spring runoff. The mud sucks at our feet and I lose a tennis shoe. A faint whiff of rotten eggs rises from the anaerobic muck. The river deepens and the watery passage opens into a small bay. I displace a flotilla of mallards as I guide the craft to shore.

Our landing spot is where the corner-notched chocolate arrowheads came from. We sit on the low riverbank, enjoying the weather. We pop a beer. A red-tailed hawk cries from a nesting site deep in the hardwoods. I tell Marc some of the history of the brown arrowheads with the corner notches and the other artifacts from this area. It started in the 1950s when I came here with my middle-school friend Roger, with whom I shared lots of archaeological adventures. One time out here, Roger, who was walking behind me alongside the river, picked a giant chocolate, side-notched arrowhead out of my boot print—an oversight for which I would take gobs of shit. That same huge arrowhead, incidentally, accompanied me to Vietnam as a talisman; it worked, protecting me from thousands of enemy bullets. It's my only aboriginal possession exempt from my self-imposed repatriation rule.

I show Marc the chert nodules, the material—called Bayport—from which the chocolate arrowheads were flaked. Several fragments of these six-inch, melon-shaped, chalk-covered concretions lie scattered over the mud, left behind by ancient tool knappers. The source of these chert nodules is in limestone bedrock that outcrops along Saginaw Bay, another thirty miles downstream. But all these particular corner-notched arrow-heads are so similar in shape, material, and flaking technique that I think they came from a single cache, meaning a whole bunch of arrow points, perhaps made by the same flint knapper, intentionally stashed together. Roger and I had found a couple of these caches and sometimes there were as many as a hundred triangular arrowheads, often accompanying a burial.

The lecture drones on, made more palatable by the fact that we are on our third beer and that Marc is actually interested in how these long-vanished folks lived. The corner-notched arrowheads were made by prehistoric hunters and gatherers who lived and fished along the rivers and the shores of the Great Lakes at least three thousand years ago—a carbon 14 sample from a red-ochre burial, which I found a mile from here when I was sixteen, dated thirty-seven hundred years ago. The low sand ridges around here at 595 feet elevation above sea level are ancient, stranded, postglacial beaches of the Great Lakes; people camped along them and buried their dead in the sandy ground.

A small shudder creeps up my spine as the mixed passions come racing back. Roger and I made the headlines of the Saginaw News when we were both fourteen. We had discovered an ancient burial about four thousand years old, a skull complete with copper beads and tools for the afterlife: a foot-long harpoon, double-tapered copper awls and axes, all covered with sacred red ochre. The copper stained everything—even the bones—green. Nearby, other human burials were found, along with incredible grave offerings—the cache of a hundred triangular arrowheads, turkey-tailed spearheads, a block of obsidian probably from Yellowstone, and polished, drilled effigies of birds. The bird-stones are atlatl counterweights; the copper tools were cold-hammered out of bedrock found up on the Keweenaw Peninsula of Lake Superior; and the flint for the turkey tails came from Flint Ridge,

Ohio. It was an ancient burial ground supplied by an extensive trading network.

I can still taste the thrill of that wonderful, exotic teenage discovery, how we walked those low sand ridges under the blazing hardwood trees of autumn and stumbled across a large anthill colored red with green grains of sand streaking the sides. Directly underneath, we knew, was a red-ochre burial with copper tools as grave offerings. You never quite lose this youthful lust for buried treasure. I still dream about finding delicious ancient artifacts buried in the ruins of my mildly apocalyptic nightmares. But dreams drift with time and now I wanted all such treasure to remain in the ground. The last thing I wanted to do was to dig up another burial.

Several items in the bag—the turkey-tail spearhead, the copper beads, and a slate pendant—probably accompanied another burial, even though they had been found apart in the sandy corner of a bean field a quarter mile north from where we are drinking beer. The reason I think they're funeral offerings is that there are traces of red ochre on all three artifacts. These, I tell Marc, will have to be reburied carefully in the woods, opposite the sand lens in the corner of the bean field.

Though the postglacial beaches carry geologic names— Algonquin Lake, Lake Nepessing, Algoma—the people who left the arrowheads here don't have modern tribal affiliations, like Sauk or Chippewa. They lived in a period of prehistory, about five thousand to nearly three thousand years ago, called the Late Archaic. You can tell this because there's no pottery scattered about with the flakes and broken rocks—meaning these people lived here before agricultural times. Pottery and agriculture came to this part of Michigan about 1,000 BCE, maybe a bit later. The first ceramics that show up here are thick and crude and are soon replaced in the archaeological record by the finer pottery of the Mound Builders, the Hopewell people who grew corn here about the time of Christ. There used to be one of these mounds just a couple of miles downriver by Green Point, but the earthwork was out in a cornfield and it got leveled by a century of plowing.

We get back to work. From the oiled canvas sack, I pull out the bags of artifacts that need to be returned to this stretch of river. Inside are lots of arrowheads but no stone axes. I've never found any here. In fact, I've only found a few of them in my life. These ground-stone tools are pretty rare.

I dump out the contents of the bag. Among the corner-notched blades is a smaller type of arrowpoint: narrow and thick with crudely flaked stems. These are an older type and were made by fishermen who hunted and gathered along the beaches of the Great Lakes. We split up the arrowheads and head out in opposite directions along the river. I dig a two-foot-deep hole in the undisturbed soil lying between the Shiawassee and the bean field and carefully place each artifact along the bottom. Two hundred yards downstream, Marc squats over his own hole.

We work quietly. After ten minutes, I get up to stretch my old back. A pair of wood ducks cruise the shoreline. Farther out are pintails and mergansers, red-necked ducks, smaller green-winged teal, and more mallards. From a perch on a dead tree, a great blue heron oversees it all. There are more species of duck and waterfowl here than I can ever identify; among my friends, the most astute duck-watchers (and best bird cooks) tend to be bird hunters so crazy you find them out here at dawn in the wintertime, wiping sleet off their shooting glasses with frozen fingers.

It's time to rebury the last artifacts that belong here—the red-ochre-stained turkey tail, the pendant, and the copper beads—which I suspect came from burials plowed up in the sandy bean field. We throw on small backpacks and push through a fringe of willows into the forest. The woods are full of songbirds: robins, kinglets, a cardinal, and choruses of unknown kinds of warblers singing from invisible perches. Thorn trees grab at our shoulders and nettles tug at our ankles. Three white-tailed deer, two does and a yearling, bolt from a thicket. We arrive at the edge of the woodlot.

A stone's throw away, a blond lens of beach sand runs across the black soil. A pair of mourning doves pick through field stubble. Before this field was cleared and plowing began, this slight rise was probably a prominent sand ridge a few feet higher than the surrounding river bottomland.

Within ten miles of this fence line, at least a hundred individual sand hills and ridges rise from the level countryside. Some are just rises, hills a few feet high; other ridges snake for hundreds of yards across the land, ten or fifteen feet above the subdued topography. All these sand landforms are remnants of postglacial lake beaches. Most of the larger sand features have been destroyed. The smaller ones often have houses built on them. The sand beaches were all full of archaeology—village sites, artifacts, and thousands of ancient burials, typified by red-ochre and copper offerings. Only a mile from the Flats, there were six stillborn children wrapped in copper beads buried along a sand ridge. Today, almost all these sand features have been bulldozed flat, removed for fill or cement, or used in construction—gone. So what? That's to be expected, I'm told, the price of progress.

But the little boy who lives in me shakes a tight fist in anger. Those ridges represented an entire universe of wonder for the fourteen-year-old. Coming back to Michigan from Montana, I rented a car to look around the landscape of my youth and rebury the arrowheads. The city had crept out over the countryside, swallowing and covering archaeological sites. I could live with the creep, but not the wholesale destruction of all the sand beaches. I winced with loss when I drove past the empty landfill pits. For me, it resembled the loss of wilderness—clear-cutting a rainforest, damming a wild river, or open-pit mining in a wilderness mountain range—a dirge for a dirt pile.

Back at the canoe, we check the canvas bag: We've reburied 90 percent of the artifacts. We climb in, push off, and head downstream, into the wildest part of Shiawassee National Wildlife Refuge to repatriate the rest of them.

Here, the Flats spread out into a wilderness of cattails and waterways. A muskrat dives and swims away. We can see the backs of huge carp plowing the edges; some of these carp grow as big as my leg. Carp are regarded as trash fish and often treated brutally by the locals, including young boys like I once was. But once I caught one by accident on a stiff rod and was surprised how strong the fish was and how long it fought. I bet carp out of clean water could be a culinary opportunity. It's not the fish's fault they were introduced here into rivers already trashed by industrial pollution. The poisoned Flint River dumps into the Shiawassee just a mile downriver from where we launched our canoe. Our take-out place, a couple more miles downriver, will be the junction with the Tittabawassee River, recipient of forty-five years of toxic dioxins flushed in upriver by Dow Chemical.

I give the canvas bag a gentle kick, only a few artifacts remain: Our mission is almost complete. We paddle down a wide channel with Canada geese honking at us from both banks. Off to the north, a bald eagle soars over a mosaic of winding waterways embedded in a matrix of bulrushes, terrifying a flock of mallards. Something flushes a pair of hen pheasants out of the reeds near the bank. I steer the canoe into shallow water at the edge of an adjacent forest and we get out.

We empty the bag. A number of big, black, roughed-out blades tumble out along with arrow points, scrapers, and a beautiful, long, coal-black spearpoint. The black material is chert, not obsidian, from the Bayport formation but highly selected by the ancients for this uncommon color, usually found only at the

Canadian geese, *Branta canadensis*, on
the Shiawassee River, Saginaw County,
Michigan. DAVID STIMAC

center of the nodules. It dawns on me that this boy scientist missed another archaeological connection—the abundance of black chert and this particular spot. What was going on here?

I remember another rare cache of roughed-out Bayport blades that I found right here. I was sixteen and hunting pheasants and ducks in the cattails. I walked over to the river and saw a pile of rocks half-submerged in the water. I discovered forty-some fist-sized chert rocks that had been tightly stacked in a pile. All were brownish Bayport chert and had been rough-flaked into fat blades. As a teenager, I thought the cache was a great archaeological discovery, so I took a fuzzy picture with a borrowed camera, hauled the entire batch of flaked stones out, and gave it to a famous archaeologist at the University of Michigan. I never heard anything of it again. I could kick myself; I want them back. I want to put them in the ground right here.

The flow gains strength and the river picks up speed. Well, at least it's the strongest, fastest current we have paddled—pretty good by Lower Michigan standards, but it wouldn't matter much if you left your life preserver behind. The canoe slides alongside a low bank at eyeball level on the left. We're not supposed to be looking but we can't help peeking at fire-cracked rocks and the occasional hammerstone on the narrow beach above. A suspicious long, dark stone catches my eye. I break and swing the canoe hard against the bank. Marc jumps out and runs back upstream. He bends over, belts out a truncated hoot, and holds up an eight-inch-long stone ax over his head. The ax is bigger and better than any such artifact I've found in my life.

We sit quietly on the riverbank and pass the exquisite artifact back and forth. This, I think, is the find of a lifetime. A cicada buzzes from a small oak behind us. I hear ducks moving out in the marsh. Solemn moments pass.

In a blaze of energy, Marc grabs the shovel and sprints up the riverbank. He chops a deep hole in the bottom of the river and sticks in the ax. Marc steps from the river and looks back, as if regarding his work. I am proud of my cousin. At another time, he might have taken the ax home. We both would have.

My cousin is a naturalist and writer, a bold activist willing to risk his ass to ease the plight of modern Indigenous people. He is a student of the historic tribes of the area. It is no accident he was my choice for an accomplice on this no-doubt illegal journey down the river to trespass and rebury the arrowheads. This is our heritage.

A few years back, I received a Guggenheim and a Lannan Foundation fellowship for "Repatriation," which helped pay for my plane ticket from Montana to Michigan. I craved a path to the sacred. The birds led the way, Marc copiloting in the bow. Our love for the Flats runs deep. Along with an old Boy Scout camp up on Beebe Lake, it is one of the magic touchstones of our respective lives. We brought—in decidedly different decades— our first loves out here. My father's ashes live in these waters.

From here on downstream, the Shiawassee becomes a real river—the Cass River dumps in on the right, the mighty Titta-bawassee on the left. Coming around the bend, we can see the Green Point take-out where we will wait for our ride. Fortunate-ly, we have a few beers left.

THE PERFECT BAIT FOR AN OUTBREAK

Fifty years ago, when I began my advocacy for grizzlies, Yellowstone's bears were in worse shape than Glacier's and I focused more on the isolated population around Yellowstone Park. My work consisted of advertising the plight of our surviving grizzly bears through public lectures, radio, or television appearances—when I could, I would bargain my way onto national news programs by using my hard-earned, growing archive of wild grizzly film footage—and championing grizzly bear protection.

Though humans killing grizzlies is always a major concern, my main message was that big wilderness areas—and connecting them—was what was most needed for survival: Survival of viable grizzly populations and nearly every other mammal species I could think of depended on wild habitats. Almost every creature evolved in habitats where adverse human influence was weak or absent—another way of defining wilderness. Of course, that's changed today, and Yellowstone was where my awareness hardened toward dogma: Most species of wild animal are eligible

Previous spread: Doug and his daughter, Laurel, take in the view of Glacier National Park from Scalplock Lookout, Montana, 1982. PEACOCK FAMILY COLLECTION

Above: A lone gray wolf howls on a rainy day on the Alaskan tundra. FLORIAN SCHULZ

for an endangered species listing today because their habitats are disappearing. Unofficially, but unmistakably, that list would include *Homo sapiens*.

We saw it coming. Close to home, throughout the Yellowstone ecosystem, winter temperatures had been rising, first recorded in 2002. By 2007, up to 95 percent of all the mature whitebark pine trees died. The dead needles turned the tops of the mountain around Yellowstone red. Only ghost forests were left.

Whitebark pine is a western, five-needle, high-altitude, stone pine whose cones produce the high-energy nuts (52 percent fat by weight) bears prefer. Red squirrels cache the pinecones, saving the bears tons of work. It's well documented that when female grizzlies eat more pine nuts, they give birth to more cubs, and they are killed at a lower rate because the higher, remote location of whitebark tree stands keeps the bears from wandering down out of the park where they run into hunters and livestock. Female grizzlies use pine nuts more than males.

Whitebark pine trees have died due to an insect infestation by the mountain pine beetle made possible by global warming. Rising winter temperatures allow the pine beetle larva to overwinter (a few nights of 30 to 35 degrees Fahrenheit below zero, depending on the insulating thickness of the bark, kills the bugs). When summer comes, adult beetles attack and larvae feed in the cambium layer, girdling the trees and sealing their doom. Young whitebark pine trees don't get infected; these small trees (less than about five inches in diameter) will simply not sustain outbreak populations. But they also don't grow cones: Whitebark pine trees may take many decades to begin cone production.

Climate change challenges all species. With record heat and drought, wildfire has reduced the carrying capacity of the Yellowstone ecosystem, diminishing the food available to all animals. After severe fires, some forests are forever changed, even being replaced by grasslands. Out-of-control, California-type wildfires are expected in the Rockies any day now, maybe this summer. Looming over all of us is the rising temperature of the planet, currently estimated at approaching 2 degrees Celsius above the baseline at the beginning of industrial emissions— around 1750.

Feeding this global fever has been relentless emissions of greenhouse gases, especially carbon dioxide. Methane, a more powerful greenhouse gas, at least in the short run, is rapidly boiling out of the thawing permafrost of the Arctic, Siberia, Alaska, and the continental shelf of the ice-free Arctic Sea. Methane release happens fast, and the warming response should be expected to be abrupt.

Methane emissions could tip us over the edge. The commonly known sources of methane are leaks from energy production and cow burps. The mainstream press hardly mentions methane coming out of the warming Arctic, from the thawing permafrost and out of the continental shelf of the Arctic Sea, now exposed to the sun by the lack of ice. Additionally, the intense wildfires across Siberia and the rest of the Arctic in June 2020 released more greenhouse gases into the atmosphere than any other month in eighteen years of data collection, according to a report cited by the *New York Times*. The same fires thawed vast regions of permafrost that will put out more methane.

There are climate change feedback systems: The big ones are on the poles. In the Arctic, where the temperature rise is more rapid than anywhere on Earth, the loss of sea ice has been extreme and extensive. By September, the sea is clear of ice far past the extension of the continental shelf; thus, sunlight is absorbed not reflected, and that layer of heat thaws more ice and melts the permafrost, which then emits more methane.

In Antarctica, warming ice sheets are beginning to break up or collapse, especially in West Antarctica, and these gigantic sheets hold back the glaciers that would run rapidly into the ocean. Along the edge of West Antarctica, warm water from depth is melting the ice shelves from the underside, contributing to sea rise. Farther east, the Ross Ice Shelf, the largest ice shelf in Antarctica, floats above the sea and is melting and breaking up from surface heat. Should the Ross collapse, as it has, partially, in recent geologic history, the sea level rise would be up to five meters, or about sixteen feet. The potential of a dozen feet of sea rise at any time should terrify coastal-city dwellers or people living in low-lying areas like Bangladesh or Florida.

From the interface of humans and animals in deforested, overhunted habitats now degraded by climate change creep an endless emergence of deadly zoonotic diseases. The Spanish flu of 1918, HIV, and SARS jumped from animals like bats, chimps, and birds to people. The scary zoonotics are viruses of the RNA variety, which can mutate and adapt rapidly. We can expect more of them as roommates for the rest of our time on this overcrowded planet. COVID-19 is one of these.

The current coronavirus—though not to diminish its singular and deadly horror—is a good example. The emergence of this particular pandemic is thought to have involved bats, bushmeat, and wet markets. We could see this one coming: The perfect storm of 7.8 billion people on Earth, the fragmentation and destruction of habitats drawing humans and animals into increasing contact, and the relentless, irreversible warming of the planet—we witnessed those thunderheads taking shape.

Doug Tompkins warned us long ago that climate change would subsume all other human issues, social or otherwise. And David Quammen told us in his fearless 2012 book *Spillover* what was coming and that this coronavirus was probably just one virus in a long line waiting in the wings to hop onto the most abundant available host—the ideal bait for an outbreak—*Homo sapiens*.

If we could see the spillover coming, why couldn't this chain of infection be interrupted? That's a tough one. Assuming the reservoir is an African or Chinese bat hitching a ride on a pangolin or bushmeat headed for a wet market in China, where do we start? I know from Round River Conservation Studies, which has had student programs in Botswana and other parts of Africa for many years, that stopping wildlife poaching for bushmeat has proven heartbreaking. The wild-animal counts are down by maybe three-quarters, presumably because of illegal hunting, and the top-down approach of much-touted armed rangers and aircraft to bust poachers has failed. With national governments depending on tourism to bring in the big bucks, village communities are mostly left out, poor and hungry. The bushmeat hunters come out of the communities where there is little enthusiasm for turning in poachers. The poached game is trafficked with legal meat coming from game farms. Bushmeat feeds workers at Chinese-owned gold and diamond mines in Africa or is moved out to wet markets, characterized by the sale of live or dead animals of most any species, many located in Asia.

Wet markets are not confined to Asia. The United States has hundreds; eighty are in New York. The ones that sell wildlife, alive or dead, are where zoonotic crossovers may happen. Wet markets are vulnerable; with massive worldwide pressure, we could get rid of them. The pictures of dogs and cats hanging with civets and chimps, dripping bodily fluids in a filthy stall, gets public attention. But cruelty does not stop at the domestic fence line. Human greed has driven such brutality into the last wild nooks of the planet.

The current pandemic will not be our last plague and it is a prime symptom that our center is not holding. Our smug assumptions of the primacy of our civilization are coming apart. Humans are not in control of the world we live in. We are not in charge.

California wildfires as seen from space.
NASA

Wildfire is everywhere, burning trees and releasing record carbon emissions: the boreal forests across Siberia and Alaska, the criminal fires in the Amazon, the fires of denial in Australia, and the unstoppable fires in our own Lower 48.

Related are rising temperatures in grain-producing regions of the world, mainly North America and Asia. These crops could fail any season now, resulting in worldwide famine. Starving people would want to get the hell out, go someplace north where they could grow food. Since humans occupy virtually every fertile chunk of ground on Earth, conflict is unavoidable. Wars will break out. Along with pestilence, this sounds like a warning from the New Testament.

Cattle are a worldwide curse. Besides the methane they produce, cows are an excuse for burning the Amazon, the loss of which, many think, will be the tipping point for the global carbon exchange keeping the planet alive.

We have not told ourselves the truth. Because it was everyone's job, it was no one's job.

There is so much beauty in the world; all we have to do is stick around to see it.

For a father who loves the Earth and finds joy in defending wild landscapes, considering our demise as a species is not a pleasant exercise. But we need to see the truth, the raw, unvarnished truth. Science and journalism water down the severity of a changing climate and pull their punches. When we try to extract the most credible science from each, we find much of it filtered through caution and timidity. There are semantic arguments that optimism and hope will color a rosier world, but how we feel about it does not change that unpolished truth.

What about temperatures too hot for life on Earth? Or habitats too impaired for survival? Some places on Earth, like Australia, are approaching 1.5 degrees Celsius above baseline, and the Arctic is 5 degrees above. The highest temperature modern humans have ever experienced over 315,000 years on Earth is about 3.3 degrees Celsius above baseline; much higher and human survival on this planet will resemble an experiment in a caged-rat lab.

"That which evolves does not persist without the conditions of its genesis" is a sentence I've found myself repeating monotonously throughout the decades. When I first wrote that line in a Glacier National Park fire lookout in the 1970s, I was thinking about habitat, especially grizzly bear and human habitat, which I considered the same—the mingled fates of humans and bears.

For the first three hundred thousand years of our time on Earth, human intelligence was carved in habitats whose remnants today we would call wilderness. Only in the past fifteen thousand years have we modified that wilderness, first with the extinction of the great late Pleistocene megafauna, and then with the rise of agriculture from multiple origins around the globe in the last ten thousand years. For over 95 percent of our time on Earth, human evolution, organic intellectual evolution, was honed in that preagricultural landscape, owing little or nothing to our time on farms or in cities. That relationship is something I don't want to gamble on—the fight to preserve wilderness is still primary.

That late Pleistocene megafauna extinction in North America was the result of climate change (the Pleistocene warming pales in comparison to the rising heat today) combined with human activity, namely overhunting, around fourteen to sixteen thousand years ago. This is the same deadly duo threatening us today—climate change and the destructive lie of endless economic growth on a planet with finite resources.

The temperature (the Bølling-Allerød warming lasted from 14,700 until about 12,700 years ago) had been rising since about twenty thousand years ago and the hunters were called Clovis people. The Clovis, known by their characteristic spearpoints and a Montana child-burial, arrived in the Lower 48 a little more than thirteen thousand years ago. Seafaring people likely arrived south of the ice via the northwest coast maybe fourteen thousand five hundred years ago, but there is no evidence they had a visible impact on the land or even survived to meet up with Clovis.

The Clovis big-game hunters, whose distinctive technology was probably developed south of the ice, came down the ice-free corridor from Alaska, as evidenced by elk-antler tools. Elk came across from Siberia around 14,700 years ago and then waited for the corridor to melt and grow sufficient vegetation to support their migration south. They certainly didn't swim down the coast. Elk apparently preceded the Clovis people by hundreds of years; why the Clovis people waited so long to come down (they could have survived in the periglacial narrows by waterfowl hunting and by packing pemmican with dogs before the corridor was vegetated) is a mystery. I suspect an abundance of Pleistocene lions, big saber-toothed cats, and short-faced bears. But the Clovis successfully exploded across North America, and in a few hundred years, left their fluted projectile points all over the land, including at a dozen or so mammoth kill sites. Had lots of scavenging, short-faced bears been around, it would have been very hard to secure a mammoth kill on open ground. Then they were gone, not the people but their way of life, in just several hundred years. Many large species of American mammals disappeared with Clovis. I record this period with envy: I can't imagine a more vibrant time to be alive in North America.

When it is indeed our time to walk offstage with the mammoths, what might be the measure of our character at the end of our tour? After peering into the abyss, how do we behave? There is great joy in doing the toil of the world, fighting for wild causes, saving pieces of the magnificent natural world.

There's plenty of work; do your job with decency and an open heart. Love your brothers and sisters in all actions, in all relationships. Speak the truth. Extend your innate empathy to distant tribes and strange animals. Arm yourself with friendship and love the Earth. Remember your elders: Walt Whitman said, "Resist much, obey little." Or, as Ed Abbey noted, "A patriot must always be ready to defend his country against his government." Hold nothing back. Join the tribes in their dignified defense of Native rights: An Indigenous viewpoint should replace all notions of Western wildlife management. Respect this militant resistance and embrace the necessity of civil disobedience. What's right isn't always legal and vice versa. Consider getting arrested.

Who and what is at risk? If past extinctions provide guidelines, then it's all life larger than a small meadow mouse. Now I can unpleasantly anticipate being among those minority humans left on Earth to die from old age. I'd be happier if everyone could. It's the scourge of my geezer-hood; I am unconcerned with my own death and fatally engaged in the lives of all my survivors. There's a bottomless, contradictory sadness in a fleeting glimpse of justice—nature bats last avenging the scorched Earth, payback to *Homo sapiens*—bundled up in the loss of beauty and suffering in the lives of the people you love most.

But then, I watched a Glacier grizzly walking slowly through a herd of elk that paid him no mind nor got out of his way. And that other grizzly that nursed her cub next to my daughter, Laurel, and me. Or, one winter, finding a roost of eight long-eared owls perched in a desert oak tree. And my pleasure when the owls returned to the same tree the next year. Seeing an old photo of my father with my two- and four-year-old children soaking in a warm creek in Yellowstone, a swell of love and loss. We visited Ed Abbey in the spring. The trace of the Growler Wash was a ribbon of gold from the globe mallows seeded by winter rains. Later, Rick Ridgeway and I drove through a field of person-high red mallow in the same landscape, with clouds of beautiful butterflies magically boiling out of the thicket. Coming over a huge dune on Namibia's Skeleton Coast with Andrea and my son, Colin, we stumbled across a hidden lake settled below the swallowing sand dunes, hundreds of pink flamingos shifted in an oasis, a high-stepping ballet of color. Back on the mesas above Arizona's Aravaipa Creek, my cowboy year, riding my sturdy horse, Hook, with my loyal collie, Larry, by my side, startling herds of dozens of mule deer and javelina every few miles—running into a hundred hoofed animals on an average day. Much later, Dennis Sizemore nervously guiding our bush-vehicle through a maternal herd of aggressive, protective elephants somewhere in the Okavango Delta. Hiking with Terry Tempest Williams up Mill Creek in Utah and finding a green-painted Kokopelli hidden in a recess. At sunset, with Ed Gage in the Bosque del Apache on the Rio Grande, we squatted in the cattails while hundreds of red-winged blackbirds slammed into the bulrushes at eyeball level. My son, Colin, and I, abandoned in northwest Namibia, with a safari vehicle in a rhino preserve, finding our water in tinajas, the same as in our own deserts, sleeping in a tent, faces toward the rear so a lion wouldn't drag us into the bush or a hyena wouldn't bite our faces off. It was Out-of-Africa-type camping and we started our evening meal in the midafternoon, a *potjie* pot (a three-legged Dutch oven), a vessel we fired with acacia chips, covering the gemsbok shank, onion, and garlic with lots of cheap South African red wine, then climbing to the top of a pass toward an unmapped trail-less valley. At the pass, the ground was ripped apart from rhino pawing. Out of the nearby towering acacia treetops rose nine giraffe heads. We went no farther, turning back toward our dinner. Once, taking Doug Seus to the Grizzly Hilton and the two of us watching a circle of friends tightly gather around a small water hole: four swaying adult mother grizzlies, four bear cubs, a yearling, and two subadult grizzly bears, a prior litter of one of the moms.

Science doesn't admit this spectrum of behavior: The bears were dancing.

It was worth it.

Opposite: The bears were dancing. Finland brown bears. Eastern Finland. VALTTERI MULKAHAINEN

Following spread: Doug warms by a rare campfire during spring in the Yellowstone backcountry, Montana, 1977. PEACOCK FAMILY COLLECTION